PENTABUS
RURAL THEATRE COMPAI

HERE I BELONG

by Matt Hartley

Here I Belong was first performed at Bromfield Village Hall,
Shropshire, on Wednesday 12 October 2016

Here I Belong

by Matt Hartley

Cast

Nathalie Barclay
Beatrice Curnew

Creative Team

Director — Elizabeth Freestone
Designer — Ellan Parry
Lighting Designer — Johanna Town
Composer & Sound Designer — Helen Skiera
Movement Director — Kitty Winter
Voice & Accent Coach — Emma Stevens-Johnson
Production Manager — Tammy Rose
Technical Stage Manager — Sam Eccles

Special thanks to:

Stella from the Land of Lost Content, Stage Electrics, Lesley Gaukroger for the costume alterations, and Alex Law for the cakes.

Tour Dates 2016

12 October | Bromfield Village Hall | Shropshire
13 October | Bromfield Village Hall | Shropshire
14 October | All Stretton Village Hall | Shropshire
15 October | Quatt Village Hall | Shropshire

19 October | The Talbot Theatre, Whitchurch | Shropshire
20 October | Hereford College | Herefordshire
21 October | Age UK Performance, The Wildlife Centre, Shrewsbury | Shropshire
22 October | Leintwardine Community Centre | Herefordshire
23 October | Chelmarsh Village Hall | Shropshire

26 October | West Deeping Village Hall | Lincolnshire
27 October | Bishampton Village Hall | Worcestershire
28 October | Ombersley Village Hall | Worcestershire
29 October | Calver Village Hall | Derbyshire

1 November | Rawtenstall Library | Lancashire
2 November | Garstang Library | Lancashire
3 November | Clayton Green Library | Lancashire
4 November | Ormskirk Library | Lancashire

10 November | Masonic Hall, Kirkby Stephen | Cumbria
11 November | UTASS, Middleton-in-Teesdale | County Durham
12 November | Bardon Mill & Henshaw Village Hall, Hexham | Northumberland

14 November | The Bikeshed Theatre | Devon
15 November | The Bikeshed Theatre | Devon
17 November | Gidleigh Village Hall | Devon
18 November | Stockland Village Hall | Devon
19 November | Lee Village Hall | Devon

22 November | St Anne's Arts & Community Centre | Devon
25 November | The Tolmen Centre | Cornwall
26 November | Blisland Village Hall | Cornwall
27 November | Nancledra Community Hall | Cornwall

CAST

NATHALIE BARCLAY | Dorothy, Marion, Scarlett, Katie
Nathalie trained at Mountview Academy of Theatre Arts.

Theatre includes: *Positive* (Park); *The Class Ceiling* (Southwark Playhouse); *Chapter 2* (New Diorama); *Much Ado About Nothing* (New Wimbledon Theatre Studio); *Consolation* (Théâtre Volière); *Positive* (Waterloo East Theatre/ Edinburgh Fringe); *A Gaggle of Saints* (The Albany); *The Boy Who Never Learned To Fly* (Arcola); *You Once Said Yes* (Nuffield); *Indian Summer* (White Bear); *Breaking News* (Cockpit); *Macbeth* (Lion and Unicorn); *Grotto* (Old Red Lion) and *Fire Island* (Charing Cross Theatre). Film includes: *Arnika* (Théâtre Volière); *New Year's Resolution, Gradulthood* (Will Hall-Smith); *50 Year Valentine* (EmJay Productions); *Awakening* (Canted Image Productions).

BEATRICE CURNEW | Elsie
Theatre includes: *A Haunting* (King's Head); *Rosa Luxembourg* (Sphinx Theatre/ NT Shed); *Pig* (Arcola); *Office Christmas Party* (Hull Truck); *The Company Man, The Madras House, Scenes from a Separation* (Orange Tree); *The School for Scandal, Dr Faustus* (Greenwich/Stage on Screen); *Burial at Thebes* (Nottingham Playhouse/ US tour); *About Tommy* (Southwark); *Hippolytus* (Riverside Studios) and many touring productions. TV includes: *The Last Panthers* (Sky Atlantic); *Black Mirror, Top Boy* (Channel 4); *Big School, Doctors, EastEnders* (BBC); *How We Invented the World* (Nutopia); *Emmerdale* (ITV). Film includes: *Writer's Retreat, Youth, The Christmas Candle, Soho Cigarette, Skyfall, The Third Falcon, I Know What I'm Doing* and many short films.

CREATIVE TEAM

MATT HARTLEY | Writer

Matt grew up in the Peak District and studied Drama at the University of Hull. Matt's first play *Sixty Five Miles* won a Bruntwood Award in the inaugural Bruntwood Competition and was produced by Paines Plough/Hull Truck. Other work for theatre includes: *Deposit* (Hampstead); *Horizon* (National Theatre Connections); *Microcosm* (Soho); *The Bee* (Edinburgh Festival); *Punch* (Hampstead/Heat and Light Company); *Epic, Trolls, Life for Beginners* (Theatre503).

Radio credits include: *The Pursuit, Final Call* (Radio 4).

Future work includes *Myth* for the Royal Shakespeare Company in spring 2017. Matt is currently writing new plays for August 012, Hampstead Theatre, Stephen Joseph Theatre and the Royal Shakespeare Company.

ELIZABETH FREESTONE | Director

Elizabeth joined Pentabus as Artistic Director in 2012. Prior to this she was freelance, directing both new plays and classics.

For Pentabus she has directed: *The Lone Pine Club* by Alice Birch, *Milked* by Simon Longman, *Each Slow Dusk* by Rory Mullarkey, *In This Place* by Frances Brett and Lydia Adetunji, *For Once* by Tim Price, *Blue Sky* by Clare Bayley, *This Same England* with Lorraine Stanley, *Stand Up Diggers All* by Phil Porter and *The Hay Play* by Nell Leyshon.

Freelance directing credits include: *The Rape of Lucrece, Here Lies Mary Spindler, The Tragedy of Thomas Hobbes* and *The Comedy of Errors* (all for the RSC); *Endless Light* (Kali/Southwark Playhouse); *The Duchess of Malfi, Dr Faustus, The School for Scandal, Volpone* (Greenwich); *Romeo and Juliet* (Shakespeare's Globe); *The Water Harvest* (Theatre503) and *Left On Church Street* (Bridewell.)

She was a staff director at the National and the RSC and has worked as an assistant director at the Royal Court, Soho and Hampstead. She has a long association with the National Theatre Studio including three stints as Director on Attachment and one as Artist in Residence.

She trained at Rose Bruford College and at the National Theatre Studio.

ELLAN PARRY | Designer

Ellan Parry is a previous winner of the Jocelyn Herbert Award and a Linbury Prize Finalist. Previous designs for Pentabus include *Each Slow Dusk* and *Milked*. Recent designs include *Rotterdam* (Trafalgar Studios, West End); *Magna Carta* (Salisbury Playhouse); *Posh* (Nottingham Playhouse, Salisbury Playhouse); *El Nino* (Spoleto Festival, USA); the world premiere of new opera *Neige* (Grand Theatre de Ville, Luxembourg); *The Miser* (Watermill); *Noye's Fludde* (Southbank Centre, London); *Someone Who'll Watch Over Me* (The Theatre, Chipping Norton); *The Secret Marriage* (British Youth Opera); *The Fairy Queen* (Brighton Theatre Royal); *Without You* (Menier Chocolate Factory, London/Panasonic Theatre, Toronto); *Electric Hotel* (Fuel/Sadlers Wells, dir.

David Rosenberg, national tour – costume designer). Forthcoming designs include *Peter Pan* (Northcott Theatre, Exeter) and new youth opera *Landings* (Glyndebourne). Ellan trained at Motley and Wimbledon School of Art.

JOHANNA TOWN | Lighting Designer

Johanna has previously lit *Each Slow Dusk* and *Blue Sky* for Pentabus. As Lighting Consultant she has worked with Pentabus on the recent purchase of their LED lighting kit, designed to offer high production values and a low carbon footprint for lighting on village hall tours.

West End and international credits include: *Dear Lupin, Fences, What the Butler Saw, Some Like It Hip Hop, Betrayal, Speaking in Tongues, Beautiful Thing* (West End); *Rose* (National/Broadway); *My Name is Rachel Corrie* (Royal Court/West End/NY); *Guantanamo* (NY/Tricycle/West End); *Arabian Nights, Our Lady of Sligo* (NY); *Haunted* (Royal Exchange/NY/Sydney Opera House); *The Steward of Christendom* (Out of Joint/Broadway/Sydney); *Macbeth* (Out of Joint/World Tour); *The Permanent Way* (Out of Joint/National/Sydney); *Our Country's Good* (Out of Joint, Toronto, USA).

Johanna has designed lighting for the National Theatre, Chichester Festival Theatre, Sheffield Crucible, English Touring Theatre, Manchester Royal Exchange and over fifty productions for the Royal Court. She is an Associate Artist for Theatre503 where credits include *The Life of Stuff* (Offie nomination for Best Lighting Designer).

Opera includes: *Porgy & Bess* (Royal Danish Opera); *Rinaldo* (Estonian National Opera); *Carmen* and *Kátya Kabanová* (Scottish Opera).

Johanna is an Honorary Fellow at Guildhall School of Music and Drama.

HELEN SKIERA | Composer & Sound Designer

Helen was part of the original sound design team for *The Encounter* (Complicite) and performed the sound live through UK and European tours, and Broadway.

As sound designer and composer: *I Know All The Secrets In My World, The Epic Adventure of Nhamo The Manyika Warrior and his Sexy Wife Chipo, The Legend of Hamba* (Tiata Fahodzi/Tricycle/Watford Palace/UK tour); *The Magna Carta Plays* (Salisbury Playhouse); *Harajuku Girls* (Finborough); *The Dog, The Night, and The Knife, Pandora's Box, Sister Of, Miss Julie,* (Arcola); *The Boy Who Climbed Out of His Face* (Shunt); *The Last Words You'll Hear* (Almeida at Latitude); *Advice for the Young at Heart* (Theatre Centre); *The Centre* (Islington Community Theatre); *The Three Sisters, The Seagull, The Laramie Project* (GSMD); *Snow White, US/UK Exchange* (Old Vic New Voices); *Meat* (Bush); *Once in a Lifetime, The Eighth Continent, An Absolute Turkey* (E15); *Colors, The Criminals, House of Bones, Medea* (Drama Centre);

As Associate: *Adler and Gibb,* (Royal Court); *I'd Rather Goya Robbed Me of My Sleep Than Some Other Arsehole* (The Gate).

As operator: *King Charles III, Chimerica, Jerusalem, Clybourne Park, Enron.* Helen has composed and performed music for websites and cabaret/comedy ensembles; and performed live on TV with *Right Said Fred*.

KITTY WINTER | Movement Director

Kitty Winter is a movement director, choreographer and director. She trained at Laban and on the MA Movement course at the Central School of Speech and Drama.

Recent movement credits include: *Cinderella*, *A Christmas Carol* and *The Rise and Fall of Little Voice* (Derby); *Blood* (Tamasha/Belgrade Theatre Coventry); *The Kite Runner*, *Rapunzel* and *Jack* (Nottingham Playhouse); *Tiny Treasures* and *The Night Pirates* (Theatre Hullabaloo); *The Dog House*, *Women on the Verge of HRT* and *Puss in Boots* (Derby LIVE); *Swan Canaries* (Arletty); *The Magical Playroom* (Seabright Productions/Pleasance Edinburgh), *Roots* (Mercury Theatre Colchester); *Ghandi and Coconuts* (Kali/Arcola); *Dick Turpin's Last Ride* (Theatre Royal Bury St Edmunds) and *Squid* (Theatre Royal Stratford East).

Recent directing credits include: *Feet First* and *Car Story* (Box Clever); *Spinning Yarns* and *FIVE* (Theatre Hullabaloo/Theatre Direct, Canada); *The Blue Moon* (Wriggle Dance Theatre); *Anything to Declare?* (The Gramophones); *Whose Shoes?* (Nottingham Playhouse) and *Awaking Durga* (Kali/Soho).

Kitty is Co-Artistic Director of family theatre company WinterWalker, and has recently produced and directed *Three Keepers* (UK tour), *Come to the Circus* (Déda, Derby), and *The Beast of Belper* (Belper Arts Festival). You can find out more about her work at www.kittywinter.com

EMMA STEVENS-JOHNSON | Voice & Accent Coach

Emma Stevens-Johnson has worked within film and theatre for over 20 years. She began teaching accents in London in 2002.

Emma has worked on international productions such as Fernando Meirelle's *360 degrees*, the critically acclaimed films *Submarine* (Warp Film for Film4) and *Brownian Movement* (Circle Films), and Cinematics Production *The Big I Am*. She has worked for BBC Cymru *(Monsters & Aliens)*, S4C *(Jonathan)*, BBC Radio Wales and ITV Wales. She has coached actors from *Californication* (US series), *Game of Thrones*, *My Mad Fat Diary*, *Hinterland* (S4C), *Hollyoaks Later*, *Pobol y cym*, *Holby City*, *Disney* and *Spooks*. She is Voice Coach in Residence for Theatre Na n'Org, dealing with both accent and vocal issues on all productions. She has worked on many occasions for Theatre Royal Bath. Emma has also worked for Wales Millennium Theatre Company, Waking Exploits, Hijinx, Actorsworkshop, ASTL Casting, The South Wales Echo and The Western Mail.

Emma is a lecturer in Voice at The Royal Welsh College of Music and Drama. She has a Masters in Vocal Studies from Central School of Speech and Drama, a PGCE from Cardiff University and is a graduate from the Oxford School of Drama.

PENTABUS
RURAL THEATRE COMPANY

We are the nation's rural theatre company. We tour new plays to village halls, fields and theatres, telling stories with local relevance and national impact.

Over 4 decades we've produced 160 new plays, supported 100 playwrights and reached nearly a million audience members. We've won awards, pioneered live-streaming and developed a ground-breaking initiative to nurture young writers from rural backgrounds.

Over the next 4 decades we'll tour further than ever before, work with new and established playwrights, extend our Young Writers programme, and continue to bring great new plays to rural audiences.

Pentabus is a registered charity (number 287909). We rely on the generosity of our donors, small and large, to help us to make brilliant new theatre.

The best new plays are made in the countryside.

You can find out more about us at **www.pentabus.co.uk**

Artistic Director	Elizabeth Freestone
Managing Director (Maternity Leave)	Francesca Spickernell
(Maternity Cover)	Kitty Ross
Projects Producer	Jenny Pearce
Audience Development & Marketing Officer	Crayg Ward
Technical Stage Manager	Sam Eccles
Bookkeeper	Lynda Lynne
Channel 4 Playwright	Tim Foley
Associate Artists	Simon Longman
	Michael Quartey
Volunteers	Mike Price
	Stephen Abbott

Twitter @pentabustheatre
Facebook Pentabus Theatre

Pentabus Theatre Company, Bromfield, Ludlow, Shropshire, SY8 2JU

Pentabus is also supported by The Millichope Foundation

HERE I BELONG

Matt Hartley

Acknowledgements

Having had the privilege of growing up in a village, I would like to thank all those who made that possible and informed that experience. Many of whom have lent their names and experiences to this play.

Deepest thanks to the Pentabus team: Crayg, Jenny, Kitty, Sam and Tim who as well as being wonderful human beings continue to challenge the notion of what rural theatre is. To the cast and crew of the show – thank you for being so generous and bringing this story to life.

And of course Elizabeth Freestone who is the most brilliant champion a writer could ever have. Rural communities will sorely miss you, I am honoured that this is your Pentabus swansong.

M.H.

For Elsie, Marion, Helen and Eden

Characters

1953
ELSIE, *twenty-seven years old*
DOROTHY, *twenty-seven years old*

1979
ELSIE, *fifty-three years old*
MARION, *twenty-six years old*

1998
ELSIE, *seventy-two years old*
SCARLETT, *twenty-nine years old*

2016
ELSIE, *ninety*
KATIE REED, *twenty-seven years old*

This text went to press before the end of rehearsals and so may differ slightly from the play as performed.

Setting

Here I Belong takes place in the fictional village of Woodside's Village Hall. Woodside has a strong agricultural history. It is this that led to Elsie's arrival as a nineteen-year-old conscript in the WLA in 1943. Historically, the village would have had a population of around about two hundred and fifty people, with a church (C of E), a pub (The Plough), a primary school and a small shop. As of 1953, when the play starts, there were several working farms, and local businesses such as a tailor and a blacksmith. During this time Woodside would have acted as a filter for local surrounding hamlets, such as Hedgeway. It is imagined that the closest major city is thirty-plus miles away. A newer town (Newton) is built, in the late sixties, on the site of Heatherview, which is approximately seven miles away and is the closest largest urban area to Woodside.

1953

*Early morning. June 2nd. 1953. Woodside Village Hall. The
wireless plays an upbeat song.* ELSIE *is dragging a table into
position, she has clearly been moving tables for a long time and
this is the final piece of the jigsaw. Once finished,* ELSIE *stands
in the middle of the hall, planning, taking it all in, enjoying the
music as she does.* ELSIE *is five months pregnant and it is
beginning to show.* ELSIE *fetches a ladder and places it below
a beam, she then opens up a bag and takes out a roll of bunting.*
ELSIE *goes up to the ladder and, without hesitating, climbs it.
As* ELSIE *gets to the top she attempts to tie the bunting, it is
knotted.* ELSIE *smiles, it was to be expected,* ELSIE *then rests
on the ladder's seat and begins to unravel it. Eventually...*

DOROTHY (*off*). Elsie?

    ELSIE *continues to unknot the bunting.*

    (*Off.*) Elsie?

ELSIE. I'm through here.

DOROTHY (*off*). Elsie, it's Dot.

ELSIE. I can hear you.

DOROTHY (*off*). Elsie?

ELSIE. I'm through here!

DOROTHY (*off*). Oh Elsie, you've not started without me,
    have you?

ELSIE. There's a lot to be done.

DOROTHY (*off*). We agreed on half past eight and it's not even
    twenty past.

    Crashing and bashing. A curse from DOROTHY.

ELSIE. Dot, careful, don't break the door down.

DOROTHY (*off*). It's Marion's pram, the wheel's stuck!

ELSIE. Well, use the door handle, it's a pram not a tank.

DOROTHY (*off*). Oh, for heaven's sake.

ELSIE. My hands are full, wait one second and I'll get the door.

DOROTHY (*off*). No, no, don't worry about me, I'll manage. Come on... wheel...

Another crash and a bang...

(*Off.*) There we go, I'm in!

DOROTHY, *flustered, enters pushing in a pram. The pram contains a sleeping baby, Marion.*

Elsie, what are you doing up there?

ELSIE. I'm trying to put up the bunting, but whoever packed it away left it in a proper tangle.

DOROTHY. You must never go up a ladder without somebody to hold it.

ELSIE. If I survived the Blitz, I can survive sitting on a ladder.

DOROTHY *takes hold of the ladder with one hand, whilst gripping the pram with her other.*

DOROTHY. Should you even be up there in your condition?

ELSIE. It's barely three foot high. I am fine.

DOROTHY. I lost all sense of balance when I was pregnant. I walked into walls. I had to be rooted to the ground. I became as adventurous as a carrot.

DOROTHY *can't stop herself, she grips the ladder with both hands.*

ELSIE. Timber!

DOROTHY. Elsie!!

ELSIE. I'm joking, I was joking, Dot!

DOROTHY. That was not funny!!!

ELSIE. You can let go, Dot, I'm plenty capable of getting down myself. You'd be better off keeping an eye on Marion – she's probably concussed from being used to batter the door down.

DOROTHY. Oh, I'm not talking to her, right now.

ELSIE. Has she been being trouble?

DOROTHY. She may look like butter wouldn't melt right now but don't let that fool you, she's been a little monster. Up all night.

ELSIE. I'll turn the music off.

DOROTHY. No! It's the silence that keeps her awake! Music. Singing. Shouting. Crashing through doors, anything loud – not a flinch. But silence, oh she screams the place down when that sets in.

ELSIE. Good luck finding anything but silence round here.

DOROTHY. It's not a laughing matter, I've been playing Al Martino on loop all night.

ELSIE. Play her enough of his songs and she'll grow to love the peace.

DOROTHY *removes a handkerchief from her pocket and begins to energetically mop her brow.*

DOROTHY. I used to think that man's voice was sent from heaven, all along it was hell to tame this devil. Well, my love, you've got all this to look forward to.

ELSIE. That I have.

DOROTHY. What? I'm hot!

ELSIE. Maybe you should go home, you're going to be no use to me if you're this giddy.

DOROTHY. Oh I will, it's only the excitement of today catching up with me, Elsie – or maybe it's the lack of sleep, it's definitely the lack of sleep. Four nights – I've had nothing, four nights! I – all the emotions are merging into one. Oh Elsie, Elsie, Elsie.

ELSIE. I'm well aware of my name.

DOROTHY. The tables and chairs, did you get them out?

ELSIE. I've yet to meet furniture that does it itself.

DOROTHY. You've been here a long time, haven't you.

ELSIE. Only a minute or two.

DOROTHY. Oh stop, I know when you're fibbing.

ELSIE. Oh do you?

DOROTHY. You're doing it now. I know because you're not smiling – it's such an effort to make yourself look unhappy. It's why you're so terrible at cards. Such a tell.

ELSIE. There's a compliment in there somewhere.

DOROTHY. Yes, there is. You won't get it all done by yourself, will you.

ELSIE. Well, I've been doing all right. I've got the wireless playing, the bunting's out, the tables and chairs are all set up and ready –

DOROTHY. Is that where they're going?

ELSIE. Yes.

DOROTHY. Oh.

ELSIE. Dot?

DOROTHY. Nothing.

ELSIE. And I'm the terrible fibber.

DOROTHY. It looks different that's all. They normally go /

ELSIE. I know how they normally go.

DOROTHY. / along the wall or – I know you're in charge but it might be that some find that a bit of a statement.

ELSIE. It's a table.

DOROTHY. Sticklers some of them.

ELSIE. I'm not making decisions lightly, Dot. I'm incredibly aware a lot of faith has been placed in me. Betty, rest in peace, her shoes are big ones to fill.

DOROTHY. Amen.

ELSIE. And I'm extremely flattered to be the person voted in to organise such an event.

DOROTHY. Perhaps there's room for a homage, to Betty. This here, is where she'd always make a lovely centrepiece. The table with the cake, or flowers.

ELSIE. That's where the television's going, Dot.

DOROTHY. The television?

ELSIE. Yes. There's never been a television to think about before, has there? Slightly different to a cake show. Cakes don't require a power point or an aerial, do they?

DOROTHY. The television, of course, how stupid of me!

ELSIE. Being able to watch it, that's what today is about.

DOROTHY. They did choose well with you, didn't they.

ELSIE. I want to get this right.

DOROTHY. Oh, you're past that stage already. Is it Margaret Emery's television we're using?

ELSIE. Who else has a television?

DOROTHY. The big house –

ELSIE. Them aside.

DOROTHY. Margaret Emery must always be the first. First car, first television, everything first in the village. Margaret wanted the party in her house as well.

ELSIE. Fleetingly, Dot.

DOROTHY. I don't know where Margaret thought everyone was going to fit. It's a large house, yes, but not that large. Did she think the whole village could crowd into her living room? Well, it wouldn't be possible, some would have to make do with watching. It becomes as much about her as it does about the Queen.

ELSIE. She's never been nothing but kind to me.

DOROTHY. When's Margaret bringing the television down?

ELSIE. Not for a while.

DOROTHY. Scared all the kids will turn up and stare at it, get in the way.

ELSIE. Well, they would, and not just the children.

DOROTHY. I would not.

ELSIE. You would sit there and gawp at it.

DOROTHY. The 'Queen' is going to be in the room with us!

ELSIE. That's not how a television works.

DOROTHY. I know, but I never thought I would live to see such a moment! In our little hall! I don't know why I am getting so emotional.

DOROTHY *mops her brow even more fervently.*

ELSIE. You're tired. Sit down.

DOROTHY. No, no, if I do I will never get back up. And I'm here to help. Getting emotional, what help is that when there is such pressure upon you?! The weight on your shoulders, Elsie, that overwhelming pressure to get this right.

ELSIE. You've said pressure once and that was enough.

DOROTHY. Oh god, I've gone and put my foot in it! Blabbering on about pressure!

ELSIE. Well, you're right, there is a lot of pressure, this is a huge moment for me.

DOROTHY. That does not do it justice, you're the first person not born in the village /

ELSIE. Don't have to tell me, I am very aware.

DOROTHY. / who has been made Chair of the Committee.

ELSIE. If I get it wrong that's all I will be hearing.

DOROTHY. Don't be ridiculous.

ELSIE. That's easy for you to say. Born and bred.

DOROTHY. This is your home.

ELSIE. I know that.

DOROTHY. If you mess it up it will be because you messed it up, not because you weren't born and bred in Woodside.

ELSIE. That's not as reassuring as you hoped.

DOROTHY. They voted you in. You've got as much right to that title as anyone in this village.

ELSIE. Well, tell that to Mary Swan.

DOROTHY. Well, that's one grudge you will never shake.

ELSIE. The way she looks at Stanley, even to this day. On our wedding day, wearing black!

DOROTHY. I remember.

ELSIE. She said to Stanley: she's not even born here. She said that about me to him.

DOROTHY. She did, yes.

ELSIE. On our wedding day! The cheek of her.

DOROTHY. You foreigners coming in stealing our men.

ELSIE. As if she ever had a chance. Not a person in this entire village would rather her for company than me.

DOROTHY. I don't doubt it.

ELSIE. Yet to her I'm the outsider. Well, look who's organising the biggest celebration in our village's recent years.

DOROTHY. You!

ELSIE. Yes! Me, Mary Swan. The soft southerner.

DOROTHY. Nobody calls you that.

ELSIE. She probably does behind my back.

DOROTHY. Only place it's safe to do it.

ELSIE. Well, Mary Swan, when you arrive later I shall parade this bump in your face with vigour. Such vigour.

DOROTHY. So you should.

ELSIE. …No. No. No. I won't, I mustn't.

DOROTHY. Why on earth not?

ELSIE. Because I won't lower myself to her level, I am far more dignified than that.

DOROTHY. Yes, you are.

ELSIE. And besides today's a celebration. That's why I will smile and ignore her and any comments she inevitably makes.

DOROTHY. It's the Queen's Coronation!

ELSIE. Yes!

DOROTHY. The day has finally arrived. A matter of hours away.

ELSIE. Oh, don't start the countdown. We're no way near ready!

DOROTHY. Everything will get done, don't worry.

ELSIE. This is a once-in-a-lifetime moment.

DOROTHY. I don't know about that – once-in-a-lifetime – the Royals, they do appear to like dying young. You see the same thing up in Hedgeway. Every family called Shimwell. None of them ever live beyond fifty. It's all those years of keeping it in the family.

ELSIE. The Royal Family have got a way to go before they're like those Shimwells up in Hedgeway.

DOROTHY. I should hope so. You'd think with the whole world at your fingertips you could find someone outside your own bloodline, wouldn't you.

ELSIE. Why are we stood round talking about inbreeding when we've got bunting to be putting up?

DOROTHY. I'm sorry, that's my fault. I just do find it awfully odd, I love our Queen-to-be, but she has essentially married a member of her family – I've only gone and done it again, haven't I.

ELSIE. Yes, you are.

DOROTHY. Give me a task then.

ELSIE. There's a bag there. See if that's in less of a mess.

DOROTHY *takes the bag. During the following they untangle the bunting. Slowly they get further away from each other as it untangles.*

DOROTHY. Heaven help us, who packed this?

ELSIE. Is it no better?

DOROTHY. It's as if they stuffed it in blind. It only takes a minute to fold it neatly but a dozen to unpick. Nobody thinks of that at the time. They simply cram it in, don't they? Leave it to the fool who unpacks. Well, it appears I am that fool. And it smells. Elsie, it's damp!

ELSIE. Nothing that a bit of air won't fix.

DOROTHY. It must have been a while since this was last out. May even be you and Stanley's wedding.

ELSIE. There will have been something more recent.

DOROTHY. Not that I remember. I'm surprised it's been kept.

ELSIE. It's a lovely thing to keep, makes you believe a celebration's only ever round the corner.

DOROTHY. It's mostly old rags from the welcome-home party. I hear Mary Swan used a pair of her old bloomers.

ELSIE. Well, that would explain half of it.

DOROTHY. Oh, Elsie, that is awfully mean.

ELSIE. True.

DOROTHY. Well, she is terribly fat, yes.

ELSIE. Rationing never seemed to make a dent in her.

DOROTHY. No one round here went shy though. Beauty of the countryside, there's always a sheep roaming, or fruit that needs plucking. We never go wanting.

ELSIE *notices she has subconsciously rested her hand on her stomach – a new wondrous chapter.*

You're very neat. I looked like a burst bag of spuds when I was carrying Marion.

ELSIE. You did not.

DOROTHY. I did, but you're so very tidy. Radiant as well Elsie, looking very radiant. It doesn't suit all – the growing, some go ashen, but you, it really does suit you.

ELSIE. Oh, Dot, I've not come here to cry.

A moment.

When did you first feel Marion?

DOROTHY. Me, early on.

ELSIE. Five months?

DOROTHY. A bit earlier. Elsie, some feel them earlier some feel them later, it's not a worry.

ELSIE. I couldn't sleep last night.

DOROTHY. The excitement. Nerves.

ELSIE. It wasn't that. Dot, I kept asking myself when will I feel something? When will I feel my baby?

DOROTHY. The movement it will come, Elsie. Be grateful for the calm, all that kicking, it wears more than a little thin after a while.

ELSIE. ...Stanley, he doesn't sleep well. A debt to the war. But last night he was peaceful. I lay there desperate to talk to him, but not wanting to take that gift from him. So I lay there, my hand here resting as if I'm holding the baby in. Hoping and hoping for a sign of life, but nothing.

DOROTHY. Els...

ELSIE. And then I thought: far, far away there's a woman who like me can't sleep, and as with me she'll also be looking up at a ceiling, with hundreds of thoughts running through her head. As in the morning she is going to become a Queen. And I said to myself, there and then, with my hand upon my child, that will be her name: Elizabeth. For if Elizabeth Windsor can stand in front of all those millions of people and promise to lead us, then that's the name I want for my girl. And then as I lay there. I felt her.

DOROTHY. No?

ELSIE. Tiny, but I felt her.

DOROTHY. Oh, Elsie, next time please don't do that.

ELSIE. What?

DOROTHY. You made me dead nervous.

ELSIE. Me?

DOROTHY. Yes, you. Don't half take your time in the telling. If war were ever to break out again better not employ you as a messenger, be over before you'd told it begun. This is wonderful! On today of all days!

ELSIE. Yes.

DOROTHY. It's a sign. It has to be, doesn't it.

ELSIE. I guess it does.

DOROTHY. It has to be a girl. She recognised her name. Elizabeth!

ELSIE. Elizabeth.

DOROTHY. Elizabeth. It's everywhere!

ELSIE. What is?

DOROTHY. Coronation Fever. It's all that's being said on the wireless. Coronation Fever. Baby's kicking. People already five deep on the roads leading to Westminster.

ELSIE. I know.

DOROTHY. Millions more ready to gather round television screens across the world.

ELSIE *gasps, a pleasant surprise*.

What? Is she kicking?

ELSIE. Yes. Yes, she is.

DOROTHY *places her hand on* ELSIE*'s stomach*.

DOROTHY. Hello, Elizabeth.

ELSIE. When I discovered we were expecting, do you know what I did?

DOROTHY. Cried?

ELSIE. Tears came later.

DOROTHY. Were they joyful?

ELSIE. Yes, joyful.

DOROTHY. It can go the other way, you see. After the war ended and the Americans over at Heatherview went back home there were lots of tears.

ELSIE. This isn't Heatherview.

DOROTHY. I know, I know too well. Not that I ever got to go to Heatherview. Never. Not once. I heard they danced for hours.

ELSIE. Dancing was a ruse if you ask me. For men who were meant to be able to shoot straight they certainly had unsteady hands.

DOROTHY. It might have been nice to have found that out.

ELSIE. It's best left to the imagination, trust me. I prayed, Dot, when I found out I was expecting.

DOROTHY. That's not like you.

ELSIE. I know. Truthfully though, I prayed that she'll be a girl.

DOROTHY. We all have our preferences.

ELSIE. The thought of a boy, Dorothy.

DOROTHY. Oh, they're not that bad.

ELSIE. The thought of thinking he might one day see what his father saw. Or being like my brother Bernard and never coming back. I should pray for peace really, I should say keep us as we now are, the flowers blooming after the storm. But I haven't because I'm not daft: war, there will be another.

DOROTHY. Oh, let's not talk like that, on a day of celebration.

ELSIE. It is true though. There just will and no little prayer from me could ever break that.

DOROTHY. War's not all bad, I suppose, it brought you here.

ELSIE. I suppose it was a means of escape for both me and Bernard. Father knew that when we both left, we were never returning, whatever form that took. I got lucky coming here, Bernard not so.

DOROTHY. Fourteen men, more boys than men really, left here for the war. Stanley one of them. Only three came back. Not all went out of duty.

ELSIE. What are you saying?

DOROTHY. If war ever came again, I pray that day never comes, but if it did and you have a son – he would be born here, to him it might be the same as it was to those boys growing up here, like it was for you and your brother in the city, he might be one of those who wanted out. Grass is often greener.

ELSIE. But it's not.

DOROTHY. Well, that's something for them to work out. We need to change the station, this music is making you awfully maudlin. You should be telling me what Stanley said about Elizabeth, not thinking about war. Today is an historic day. A day for looking forwards not backwards. Yes?

ELSIE. Yes.

DOROTHY. Well, let's get something upbeat on.

DOROTHY *changes the station.*

There we go. Oh, I like this one. Now go on, not the bunting, tell me what Stanley said about Elizabeth.

ELSIE. I woke him after feeling her. He gave a little smile. He then got up and went to his shed.

DOROTHY. His shed, of course, he did.

ELSIE. He's started carving a crib this morning. I can't get him to stop. Leave him to it, I thought. He seems happy. He can lose himself in there for days.

DOROTHY. If only to have a man who embraced his own company rather than that of every other fool. The thought of him chiselling away.

ELSIE. He may even wear his uniform today.

DOROTHY. Oh, Mary Swan will be delighted.

ELSIE. She will. It takes a rather special occasion for that. To open those memories.

DOROTHY. This is where it all began for you, Elizabeth. Your mother and father. Tell her.

ELSIE. Talk to her?

DOROTHY. Heavens, yes. You don't talk to your baby?

ELSIE. I do.

DOROTHY. Then why would you skip this? It's a vital part of her story.

ELSIE. Did you talk to Marion about where you and George first met?

DOROTHY. The first time I saw George we were both four years old, he was perched on the wall at the top of Hanging Lane looking out over the fields. He was picking his nose. Very aggressively. It was disgusting. I told Marion many things, about the fields, the ducks on the river, about Doris Christie's incredibly poor stock selection in her shop, Tom Robinson...

ELSIE. Tom Robinson?

DOROTHY. Tom Robinson, oh yes... not just Tom. You, Mary Swan. Lots of people. But not so much about her father. I thought she could make her own mind up on that one.

DOROTHY *smiles, but it's not convincing.* ELSIE *senses it is time she changed the subject.*

ELSIE. This hall is where we met. We had our wedding reception here. Not as big a do as this but big enough.

DOROTHY *waits.*

DOROTHY. Not a big do! What a gripping tale, Elsie. Enid Blyton's shaking in her boots at the thought of the competition. Tell your daughter about the first time you saw her father.

ELSIE. Is this more for you than her?

DOROTHY. I do love romance, true, but I think talking to your child is a good thing.

ELSIE.... fine... the first time I... when the war ended, your father, he was a pilot, I should say that at the top, shouldn't I?

DOROTHY. It is a handy detail.

ELSIE.…He was a pilot, your father. He grew up here and he
    left to fight in the war. I came here from the city. I was what
    they called a land girl… His mother, your grandmother, rest
    in peace, had talked to me about him for months upon
    months. I think she saw me and the other new girls as sirens,
    praying that we'd call the men back safely home. She'd tell
    me: my Stanley he's not like the other men. He's educated.
    Bright. A pilot. Not cannon fodder. Every day he walked
    seven miles there and back to the grammar school in
    Heatherview. Before I'd even seen him it was as if I knew
    him in his entirety. And she was right, he wasn't like the
    other men. There was a welcome-home party here. For all
    those who made it back. Not many returned. But he did. I'd
    never seen your father till that day. He was sitting there.

DOROTHY *gestures to go there.* ELSIE *submits. The music
changes again, it's from a different time and place.*

He was sitting here. Under this noticeboard. Quiet as a
mouse. Half a pint in his hand. In his uniform. Pressed as if it
was new. His back was so straight, you could draw a line up
against the wall and use it to stake a sapling. He was
watching. The dancing and swaying. His village. Those he
knew. Those gaps he knew were missing. Taking it all back
in. And amongst all that calm, that stillness, I saw his right
foot tapping. And I smiled and that's when we first glimpsed
each other… He offered his hand to me and I took it. I don't
remember the eyes that inevitably watched us. His hands
rested on the base of my spine. His eyes never leaving mine. ·
And after we danced, we sat back here watching it all
unfold… Doesn't look as romantic now what with Margaret
Emery's WI notices and the bowls team sheet, but at the time
it felt like the most magic place in the world.

DOROTHY. Hear that. This isn't only where we come to play
    bridge. It's where romance breeds.

ELSIE. And parties are meant to be held.

DOROTHY. Very well, let's get this bunting up.

    ELSIE *has taken another ladder and placed it under a beam.*

ELSIE. Here. Take that end. Tie it to that. Got it?

DOROTHY. Got it!

They both go up respective ladders with the bunting.

Have you noticed a lot of women have taken it upon
themselves to repopulate Woodside of late?

ELSIE. Being one of them, I have.

DOROTHY. It is a powerful instinct. To reproduce. In times of
great loss. Lots of beds used in ways they've not been used
in years.

ELSIE. I wouldn't say that – what with all the GIs that were
roaming round here.

DOROTHY. Elsie!

ELSIE. Not to cast aspersions, Dorothy.

DOROTHY. Sometimes I do wish their were aspersions to be
cast! Instead I was at home, married to a man who was
deemed too useless to even be served up as canon fodder for
a German machine gun.

ELSIE. He was missing a leg, it would have hardly been fair to
send George.

DOROTHY. Lot of them came back missing a lot more. Hasn't
meant they've drowned themselves in self-pity. Tom
Robinson is back working Ashton Orchard, missing one
hand, still the best picker in the whole village... marvellous
picker. Even with one hand... marvellous...

They tie off the bunting.

ELSIE. Will he be here later?

DOROTHY. Tom Robinson?

ELSIE. George!

DOROTHY. Oh, there's going to be a bar, I would imagine so.

ELSIE. Dorothy, he's not that bad.

DOROTHY. I suppose he could be Edward Reed. Awful racket
from their house last night.

ELSIE. I heard. When I was young that sound would have been lost amongst many other sounds, but out here it can carry a mile.

DOROTHY. Always been rotten that family. The war made him even worse. Who boasts about taking so many lives?

ELSIE. He'll have to make amends one day.

DOROTHY. Amen to that. Sometimes I'm ever so grateful for that family, though, you know. There's a bad family in every village, Elsie. It's the way it is. Good thing is none of us are looking over our shoulder thinking it could be us. As the Reeds make it so easy. Oh, that looks lovely.

ELSIE. It's a start.

DOROTHY. A very good one.

ELSIE. Be a love and get the tablecloths that are in the kitchen.

DOROTHY *goes to the kitchen.* ELSIE *smiles, as she anticipates a reaction. A scream.*

DOROTHY. Elsie!

ELSIE. Oh hell, it's not another mouse, is it?

DOROTHY. No, there's a refrigerator in the kitchen!

ELSIE. Don't do that to me.

DOROTHY. When did that happen?

ELSIE. It arrived two days ago.

DOROTHY. Why did nobody tell me!? I knew there'd been talk of getting one. Oh my word. It is… wonderful /

ELSIE. This is probably why I didn't tell you. Wait till we're done /

DOROTHY. / How does it open… the handle, I see. /

ELSIE. / then you can spend an hour looking at it, should you wish!

DOROTHY. / It's so cold.

DOROTHY *enters, holding a bottle of cider.*

Is this John Ashton's cider?

ELSIE. Dorothy, leave the cider alone!

DOROTHY. Has he made this for today?

ELSIE. Yes, he has.

DOROTHY. Gallons of it.

ELSIE. I don't know where he gets the time? If he's not milking cows, running an orchard or pressing cider – he's delivering Marion.

DOROTHY. The man has hands fit for birthing cows not babies.

ELSIE. He was a lifesaver.

DOROTHY. I'll give him that – still I think I deserve a taste to get rid of that memory.

ELSIE. It's not even nine in the morning!

DOROTHY. When has that stopped you?

ELSIE. There'll be plenty of time for that later!

DOROTHY. All right, I've put it back.

   DOROTHY *returns to the kitchen.*

   It's so cold!

ELSIE. Then the fridge is doing its job. Close the door.

DOROTHY. All these shelves, and a light!

ELSIE. It has to be closed to work properly.

DOROTHY. That's not as much fun to look at.

   DOROTHY *comes back into the hall, struggling under the weight of a pile of tablecloths.*

   It's taller than me!

ELSIE. Yes.

DOROTHY. I don't know where a refrigerator would go in our house.

ELSIE. The kitchen would be best.

DOROTHY. It wouldn't fit!

ELSIE. There are smaller ones. It's for the hall, it needed to be large. For times when we have parties to prepare for...

DOROTHY. A refrigerator in our little hall. My oh my, how grand! We could be in the big house! They will have one that size, don't you think. Even two refrigerators perhaps. No, we couldn't possibly fit a refrigerator that size. A television we could fit. I keep asking George when will we get a television. He gives me the same answer to a car, to a refrigerator: does money grow on trees? I tell him: if it did you'd never have planted one.

ELSIE. Stanley talks of getting a car, but then I ask where would he want to go and he can't give me an answer. Let's start here.

DOROTHY *and* ELSIE *start to lay the cloths over the tables.*

DOROTHY. Have you seen the big house?

ELSIE. It's only next door.

DOROTHY. They have made a good show of it.

ELSIE. Lot of flags, that's true.

DOROTHY. They'll be going to London, I bet. Probably know the Royal family, don't they. Today must be a day for missing London, Elsie.

ELSIE *stops folding. Considers.*

ELSIE. I don't know what I would be missing.

DOROTHY. To be able to wave as she passed.

ELSIE. What good is a wave amongst so many?

DOROTHY. Oh, Elizabeth would feel it.

ELSIE. No, she wouldn't.

DOROTHY. Oh, she would.

ELSIE. What are you doing with that tablecloth?

DOROTHY *wraps a tablecloth round herself as if it's a gown.*

DOROTHY. Wave at me.

ELSIE. People are going to eat off that.

DOROTHY. Wave at me, loyal subject.

ELSIE *sighs, waves at* DOROTHY.

More vigour. Happier. That's it. Oh, she will feel all the good will, even such a half-hearted display, would inspire Her Majesty. My god, imagine if she was to fall!

ELSIE. She won't fall.

DOROTHY. But imagine! Her feet trapped in her gown.

ELSIE. I'm not going to imagine the Queen falling over.

DOROTHY. It's such a simple thing to do. Look, I caught my feet just then.

ELSIE. The Queen doesn't walk in that way.

DOROTHY. Nerves do strange things to a person.

ELSIE. She won't walk like that, or fall, Dot. Royals get taught to walk properly. Gracefully. Not a chance she'll fall.

DOROTHY. I suppose there would be many people to help steady her, in case. Elsie, imagine being on those streets, how wonderful would it be to know that something so small as a gesture could play a part in something so huge.

ELSIE. A second then she'd be past.

DOROTHY. To be part of that.

ELSIE. You've barely left Woodside, let alone gone to London.

DOROTHY. It'd be an awful adventure.

ELSIE. Trust me, you wouldn't like it.

DOROTHY. I may.

ELSIE. No member of your family has ever left here.

DOROTHY. No, my mother went to Scarborough.

ELSIE. For how long?

DOROTHY. Well… it was a long weekend. She'd booked
a return ticket so had to come back.

ELSIE. When that television shows you London, remember those
people lining the streets are dreaming of places like this.

DOROTHY. The hall?

A moment.

ELSIE. I'm older than my mother ever was, Dot. She never
ever got to see places such as this. There. London. To her the
horizon was a city of grey, of grit and grime. She was dead at
twenty-four. That was meant to be me too. But it's not
because I'm here. In this place that my mother could only
ever have dreamt of.

DOROTHY. You don't have to go far to see a lot, Father used to
say that. It'd be nice to know that for sure though, only if it
was just once.

A moment.

ELSIE. I don't want you to go.

DOROTHY. I'm not going anywhere, am I. You know that.
I know that. It's nice to have a little daydream every once in
a while though.

ELSIE. As of today the world's going to change. Twenty
million people sat round a screen, Dot. Twenty million. The
world is getting bigger not smaller.

DOROTHY. The future our children are going to have.

ELSIE. Yes.

DOROTHY. What a time to be born. Imagine all the things they
will see.

ELSIE.… Yes.

DOROTHY. The adventures they will have.

ELSIE. Yes.

DOROTHY. What a time to be alive.

ELSIE. Yes.

The music changes. It's a song they love.

DOROTHY. Oh, do you hear that!?

ELSIE. I do.

DOROTHY. I know you love this song. Let's dance.

ELSIE. The rest of the cloths, the –

DOROTHY. Can wait. Come on before the riff-raff arrive and I still have the energy. That's it.

They dance and laugh, two friends lost in a moment… the music changes.

Rock and roll.

Their dancing changes to reflect it… till…

ELSIE *is left by herself.*

ELSIE *ages before our eyes…*

1979

Woodside Village Hall.

2nd May 1979. Morning. A miserable day. Rain.

ELSIE *is now fifty-three years old and is in fine health.*

ELSIE *is wheeling in a helium canister.*

MARION *enters.* MARION *is now twenty-six years old, her style is very much an ode to Debbie Harry.*

MARION *shakes her umbrella dry.*

ELSIE. Hello there, can I help you?

MARION. Have I changed that much?

ELSIE. Marion?

MARION. Hi.

ELSIE. Oh my, Marion! I'm sorry, without my glasses all I could make out was bright blonde hair!

MARION. Know me, never happy sitting still.

ELSIE. It completely threw me! Let me put these on.

ELSIE *puts her glasses on.*

Oh yes, that is definitely you.

MARION. It is.

ELSIE. With what a bright new look.

MARION. It's been like this for months, I forget that it would be the first time you would have seen it.

ELSIE. Is this the fashion now?

MARION. In some circles. That's not the reason why I've done it.

ELSIE. Of course. Never been a sheep, have you. Well, it looks…

MARION. Good? Not good?

ELSIE. It wouldn't be for me, but on you, Marion, it is a wonder.

MARION. I'll end up changing it again no doubt.

ELSIE. Who is that singer? Is that who inspired it?

MARION. I'm not sure who you mean.

ELSIE. The blonde one, what's her name?

MARION. Blondie?

ELSIE. No.

MARION. Debbie Harry?

ELSIE. Yes, that's her name. I saw her on *Top of the Pops*.
Thought she was rather good. You're laughing at me.

MARION. No, no, Elsie, I'm not – it doesn't matter.

ELSIE. Have I said something?

MARION. Well, Elsie, we're talking about the same person.

ELSIE. Are we?

MARION. Blondie, Debbie Harry, it's the same person.

ELSIE. Oh, is that right?

MARION. Yeah.

ELSIE. She should make up her mind.

MARION. Yeah.

ELSIE. It suits you. Dynamic.

MARION. Thank you.

ELSIE. Don't let anyone else round here tell you otherwise.

MARION. I won't.

ELSIE. I much prefer it to when you had it all shaved round
the side.

MARION. …thanks.

ELSIE. We can all get it wrong once, can't we.

MARION. It's only hair. It grows.

ELSIE. Very true. Come here.

They hug. It's not as natural as it perhaps once was.

MARION. Hi.

ELSIE. Hello. It is lovely to see you.

MARION. And you.

ELSIE. You need to come back more often.

MARION. It's not been that long. I was here for Christmas.

ELSIE. How are you?

MARION. Me?

ELSIE. Yes, you.

MARION. A little wet.

ELSIE. Disgusting out there.

MARION. Yeah.

ELSIE. May!

MARION. Yeah.

ELSIE. Luckily I turned the heating on earlier!

MARION. Yeah.

ELSIE. Don't tell Claire Emery, she'll complain about the bill –
    she's not like her mother, Margaret, tight as a duck's arse,
    even in February having it on can cause a fuss, let alone
    May! I suppose it's a useful quality for the treasurer.

MARION. My lips are sealed.

ELSIE. You should go and perch by it.

MARION. I'm not too bad.

ELSIE. Your hands are telling a different story.

MARION. …Okay.

   MARION *goes towards the heater/radiator.*

ELSIE. How are you then?

MARION. Personally?

ELSIE. Yes.

MARION. In life?

ELSIE. Yes.

MARION. Great. I'm great.

ELSIE. You're making a success of London?

MARION. I am. It's great. For me. It's the only place for me to be.

ELSIE. That's wonderful, I'm so pleased for you. It can be a cruel place.

MARION. Yeah. Some say that, yeah. But not for me. For me it's all that I ever thought it could be.

ELSIE. Oh good, that makes me happy. When did you get in?

MARION. I drove down late last night.

ELSIE. You drove?

MARION. Yeah.

ELSIE. Your mother didn't say you had a car.

MARION. I hired one.

ELSIE. Hired one?

MARION. Yeah, it cost a fortune.

ELSIE. I'm sure it did.

MARION. I'm being dramatic. It wasn't that expensive. What other option did I have though? It's easier getting to the Moon than here on public transport.

ELSIE. You should have called. Stanley or I would have picked you up from Heatherview.

MARION. Very kind. Thank you.

ELSIE. If you ever need that we can. Get the train there and we can pick you up. Remember that.

MARION. I will.

ELSIE. It's the least we can do. You've seen your mother then.

MARION. I have, yeah.

ELSIE. I was with her yesterday.

MARION. She said.

ELSIE. She was having a really good day.

MARION. That day's gone then.

ELSIE. Why, what's happened?

MARION. She wouldn't get out of bed.

ELSIE. It can be hard first thing in the morning.

MARION. This was when I got in.

ELSIE. That's understandable, the illness tires her out.

MARION. Wouldn't even try this morning. I left her still in bed.

ELSIE. Peaks and troughs.

MARION. Wasn't this bad at Christmas.

ELSIE. That's the nature of it, darling, time's not out to be her best friend, but trust me, she's being very strong. How long are you staying?

MARION. I can be here for a few days, a week at the most.

ELSIE. That will be good for her.

MARION. I've not been back for that long in years. I'm crawling the walls already. I'll end up making her worse.

ELSIE. Now that is rubbish. Absolute rubbish, you hear me. Marion, do you hear me?

MARION. Yes.

ELSIE. What did I say?

MARION. You said what I was saying was rubbish.

ELSIE. And I'm right. She'll love having you home. She will. And it's important for you, whilst she's still very much your mother, because she won't always be.

A moment.

MARION. She said you would be here.

ELSIE. You've actually come to see me, have you?

MARION. It wasn't a desperate need to find out the bridge results that brought me down.

ELSIE. Well, that is nice to hear. You can help me set up.

MARION.... Okay.

ELSIE. We've got a big day ahead. Lots to be done.

MARION. Do you mean tomorrow?

ELSIE. No, no, today. First off, you can help me blow these up.

MARION. Helium balloons?

ELSIE. Yes, Ben Robinson left the canister out by the door.

MARION. Ben Robinson?

ELSIE. My own fault really, I told him to leave it there and I'd sort it and we'll need some with regular air – as they'll want a few to chase and kick about.

MARION. Do voters really want to kick a balloon?

ELSIE. Voters?

MARION. Yes.

ELSIE. I'm a little lost.

MARION. This is a serious moment in our history –

ELSIE. What are you talking about, darling?

MARION. The General Election, kicking balloons around is a bit flippant.

ELSIE. What's the election got to do with balloons?

MARION. It's tomorrow.

ELSIE. I know that.

MARION. This is the polling station.

ELSIE. Why would I put balloons out for the vote?

MARION. I don't know, I thought it was a village thing.

ELSIE. Do you think we're that eccentric out here? Kicking balloons about during a vote!?

MARION. You're not setting up for the vote?

ELSIE. A couple of booths and a table, that's all we need for that.

MARION. Then what are you doing?

ELSIE. It's Sam Robinson's birthday party this afternoon.

MARION. Sam Robinson?

ELSIE. Ben Robinson's son. He's having a party. What are you laughing for?

MARION. This is nothing to do with the Election?

ELSIE. No.

MARION. It's a child's birthday party?

ELSIE. Don't sound so surprised, you came to plenty of parties here.

MARION. Not the day before a General Election.

ELSIE. The village doesn't stop because people are ticking a bit of paper and dropping it in a box.

MARION. This is so typical of this place. A child's party.

ELSIE. That's right.

MARION. And it's for Ben Robinson's son?

ELSIE. Yes, Ben and Anne Christie's, Sam. He's turning five.

MARION. Five? Really?

ELSIE. He is.

MARION. Ben and Anne were a year younger than me at school and they've got a five-year-old.

ELSIE. Your time will come, darling.

MARION. I'm not after a time, Elsie. I'm very happy with my life. /

ELSIE. Marion.

MARION. / Being independent. /

ELSIE. Marion.

MARION. / It's my choice. /

ELSIE. Rightly so.

MARION. / No one else's.

ELSIE. I'm sorry, I certainly didn't mean to offend.

MARION. Well, you did.

ELSIE. You need to live exactly the life you want.

MARION. And I am. I am.

ELSIE. Good. That's what everyone wants for you.

MARION. Well, it's what's happening. It is. Sorry, sorry, Elsie.

ELSIE. No, it's me that should be saying that.

A moment.

MARION. This is not what I envisaged today looking like.

ELSIE. I'm sure.

MARION. You and Mum used to always be setting up something in here.

ELSIE. Your mother was always here more to chat than help. If anything this illness has been the excuse she's been dreaming of for years. Now she just sits right there and bends my ear about something, whilst I do all the lifting!

MARION. She's still coming down then?

ELSIE. Wild horses wouldn't drag her away.

A ghost walks over MARION's *grave.*

MARION. Oh god.

ELSIE. Are you okay?

MARION. I just… flashback… do you remember when you turned the hall into Father's Christmas grotto?

ELSIE. Oh, don't remind me, that is my one true disaster as social secretary.

MARION. Dad as Father Christmas, what did you expect?

ELSIE. He fitted the costume.

MARION. Nothing jolly about his gut.

ELSIE. Well, I won't let that day put me off – little Sam needs
    this to be as good as any party that this hall as ever had.

MARION. I bet he's a monster – Sam. If he's anything like his
    mother.

ELSIE. Have you not heard? Anne's done a runner.

MARION. Anne Christie has?

ELSIE. Did your mum not tell you?

MARION. No. When was this?

ELSIE. A month or so ago. Ben's doing ever so well in spite of it.

MARION. Anne's just gone?

ELSIE. Long gone. With the delivery man.

MARION. What delivery man?

ELSIE. How has your mum not told you this? It has been
    a ginormous scandal.

MARION. …We've been missing each other's calls.

ELSIE. Well, Anne was back working in her mother's shop and
    this man, Clive I believe he is called, was the man who
    dropped off all the stock. Apparently, this Clive, gave Anne a
    free sample of Arctic roll and that was that.

MARION. Elsie!

ELSIE. What?

MARION. Is that a euphemism?

ELSIE. Oh god! It wasn't meant to be, he sold Arctic rolls! But
    I guess it's another way of saying what happened next.
    Apparently, it had been going on for a good year or so. Anne
    left poor Ben a note and that was it. Poof, gone.

MARION. Bloody hell. Elizabeth once taped Anne in the box
    your washing machine came in, it took Anne four hours to
    escape from that, yet she can do a runner from her family.
    Poor Ben, poor Sam.

ELSIE. I know. He's a nice little boy, actually. Thin. Doesn't take after his grandmother in that way.

MARION. Is Mary Swan still quite fat?

ELSIE. Quite is very polite. You know your mother carried quite a torch for Ben's father.

MARION. Did she?

ELSIE. Oh yes. I don't think it was far off being mutual.

MARION. He only had one hand.

ELSIE. But it was a good one. Tom was the best picker on the orchard right up until the day he passed.

MARION. Mum never mentioned him.

ELSIE. Oh, she wouldn't, it stole a bit of her, when Tom got with Mary Swan. It was here of all places.

MARION. Here?

ELSIE. Oh yes, this hall is where many romances began or floundered. It'd been a wonderful day. The entire village had come out for the Queen's Coronation. You were ever so well behaved in the corner.

MARION. Me?

ELSIE. Oh yes, barely a peek out of you.

MARION. I don't remember any of this.

ELSIE. Of course not, you were barely a month old, which is a better excuse than most – there were a lot of sore heads the next day.

MARION. Dad leading the way no doubt.

A smile of recognition.

ELSIE. I saw Mary and Tom together before your mother did.

MARION. You actually remember it?

ELSIE. I do when I'm here. Your mother and I were dancing together. And I saw Mary over your mother's shoulder, like the shark, in that film…

MARION. *Jaws*.

ELSIE. Exactly that. Honing in. It would be fair to say, Mary
Swan was as greedy with men as she was with food. She
pounced on Tom. There was no choice on his part. And
I kept trying to swivel your mother away, make it part of the
dance, thinking any second now Tom will push Mary Swan
away. But he didn't. Or couldn't.

MARION. He needed a bigger boat.

ELSIE. I'm not sure what boats have got to do with it, darling.

MARION. It's a line in *Jaws* – doesn't matter. Forget it.

ELSIE. In the end, I couldn't keep turning your mother away
from it.

MARION. Mum was upset?

ELSIE. She ran straight out. I found her stood in the brook. I told
her it was nothing, that Tom had had no choice, but the next
thing you know Mary Swan was expecting Ben.

MARION. Mum's had a horrible life.

ELSIE. That's not true now.

MARION. She gets stuck with my dad, then finally he dies and
then she gets struck down with MS.

ELSIE. Do you know how people call round to see your
mother? Every day it's a pilgrimage. She's more popular
than Mother Teresa.

MARION. She couldn't even summon the energy to get out of
bed.

ELSIE. All is going to be well, you know that, all is going to
be well.

A moment. MARION *heads to the window and finds herself
staring out towards the big house.*

Do you remember when you and Elizabeth used to creep
over into the big house's garden?

MARION. That was a long time ago.

ELSIE. Not that long.

MARION. We were fifteen, sixteen at most.

ELSIE. What you got up to I'll never know.

MARION. We just lay on the grass. It was like velvet.

ELSIE. Oh yes, there was no smoking, no drinking, no boys –
just lying on the velvet grass.

MARION. Thought you didn't know what we got up to!

ELSIE. The pair of you would come back with scarves draped
round your neck in the height of summer, it was pretty
obvious!

MARION. Oh god… I'm cringing at the thought… they were
two brothers. It was, John that gave me the bites, no Jack,
John was who Elizabeth was with. Jack was my first kiss –
just round the back here. You don't want to hear this…

ELSIE. We're all adults here.

MARION. Their family used to camp up at Ashton's farm. Two
summers in a row. I don't remember how we ended up
meeting but… obviously Elizabeth got John as he was more
of a catch than Jack… that was all such a long time ago…

A moment.

ELSIE. The grass won't be quite the same since they moved on.

MARION. Still empty?

ELSIE. The rumours were that it was going to be turned into
a hotel. Nothing's come of that though.

MARION. Hardly the time to be setting up a hotel – state the
economy's in.

ELSIE. Is that so?

MARION. This country's doomed. It's only going to get worse
if they vote her in tomorrow…

ELSIE. Why don't you put that fire into the balloons.

MARION *nods, she then takes a balloon out of the bag and
starts to blow it up.*

Very good. A few of those and we'll be well on our way.

MARION *struggles with the balloon.*

Oh look at you.

MARION. Have I gone red?

ELSIE. You're like a lovely little Christmas robin.

MARION. Nothing lovely about robins, Elsie. Extremely
territorial. Studies have been conducted at –

ELSIE. No. I won't have a bad word said about robins.

MARION. I know they seem sweet and innocent but this study
would change your thinking.

ELSIE. My brother Bernard, who died back in the war, he's
been reincarnated as one.

MARION. Oh, right, has he now.

ELSIE. Oh, don't make that noise. I've not gone mad. Bernard
came back at first as one of the cows on the Ashton farm, but
that particular one got crushed by a tree in April when the
winds were high, which was very fitting for Bernard, with
his lack of luck. Did your mother not tell you that either?

MARION. Tell me what?

ELSIE. About John Ashton's cow.

MARION. No, she didn't.

ELSIE. It caused a fuss at the time.

MARION. I bet.

ELSIE. Four tiles blew off the church as well.

MARION. Four whole tiles?

ELSIE. One fell straight on to Margaret Emery's headstone and
cracked the top of it. Even in death she gets attention. Your
mother definitely didn't tell you that?

MARION. Not that I remember.

ELSIE. Anyway, ever since that cow got squashed this robin has
appeared. And it comes ever so close to me, as close as we
are now, and looks me straight in the eye. The way Bernard

did, no blinking and Bernard he never let me win. Never. Just like this robin.

MARION. What does Mr Rose say about this robin?

ELSIE. Stanley. He hasn't taught you for sixteen-odd years.

MARION. I know.

ELSIE. Stanley wasn't simply your teacher.

MARION. I know, but –

ELSIE. For a start he wiped your bottom many times.

MARION. That's not going to help with changing what I call him! Calling him that feels like I would be breaking some sort of rule.

ELSIE. With a haircut like that, thought you were all about breaking the rules!

MARION *looks away, uncomfortable for a second or two.*

MARION. What does Stanley say?

ELSIE. About wiping your bottom? That doesn't come up much in conversation, funnily enough.

MARION. About Bernard the robin.

ELSIE. Oh, Stanley humours me. He puts fat out there to lure the robin in, then takes photos.

MARION. He's still keen on photography then?

ELSIE. Oh yes, if Stanley's not building something with wood he's taking a photo. It suits him; the watching, the detail, the silence. Sometimes I wish it was something that took up less space. All the solutions he keeps for the photos! Blacking out the bathroom, never sure what I'm going to wee into in the night.

MARION. You could use Elizabeth's room. She wouldn't mind.

ELSIE. True, I don't think she would. Your mother has never touched your room.

MARION. And I told her to. I'm not sentimental.

ELSIE. Perhaps someone else is.

MARION. This is neither mine or Elizabeth's home any more.

ELSIE. Home doesn't have to be where you sleep at night. It can be many many things.

Where you feel safe. A sense of place. Identity. You're not going to tell me Woodside doesn't offer you that?

MARION. What answer would Elizabeth give you to that?

A moment. ELSIE *smiles, she wanders over to a photo hanging on the wall.*

ELSIE. This is actually one of Stanley's photos. And this one as well.

MARION. He's got a real eye for it.

ELSIE. It's just his hobby. Nothing to set the world on fire.

MARION. Do you know at school everyone wished Stanley was their dad?

ELSIE. I married well.

MARION. Elizabeth hated that.

ELSIE. Did she?

MARION. I never understood why. Nobody ever said the same about mine.

ELSIE. I'm sure they did.

MARION. You know they didn't. Not even me. I thought Stanley might one day leave for another school. Somewhere bigger, more challenges.

ELSIE. No, Stanley's done his travelling. He likes where he is. He can walk to work. We get our lunch together, sit by the river, watch it flow. You can't put a price on that.

MARION. How many of these do you want doing?

ELSIE. Well, it would be a miserable party with that many.

MARION *nods, fiddles with a balloon.*

MARION. How's Elizabeth?

ELSIE. Have you not seen her recently?

MARION. No.

ELSIE. Oh. You've spoken to her?

MARION. We're in different worlds these days. How is she?

ELSIE. How is she, she's focused.

MARION. Very diplomatic.

ELSIE. Elizabeth has many boxes she wishes to tick and she is
yet to tick them all.

MARION. Do you and Stanley count as one of those things?

ELSIE. That's a very silly thing to say.

MARION *feels silly for saying it, she tries to blow up
a balloon, fails.*

MARION. When did you last see Elizabeth?

ELSIE. Christmas. Not too long ago, it's when you last saw
your mother.

MARION. You don't go to London to see her?

ELSIE. We speak on the phone. I bored her senseless about
John Ashton's cow.

MARION. She'll be voting her in tomorrow, won't she.

ELSIE. Who?

MARION. Thatcher.

ELSIE. That's up for her to decide.

MARION. She will. It's what all bankers do. Thatcher's going
to tear this country apart. The way she's campaigned. It's
obvious. There's one of the posters, 'Labour isn't working',
plastered across a banner on my road, the one with people
queuing for jobs, you know it?

ELSIE. I can't say I do.

MARION. Do you know they weren't even unemployed?

ELSIE. We didn't get those posters out here.

MARION. They were actual Conservative members who had
volunteered to take part.

ELSIE. I see.

MARION. As if they know what a queue even is, let alone
a queue for a job centre! It's a fraud. Money spent on
fear-mongering and muck-spreading. Like they care about
the poor, the unemployed. But it will work won't it because
people will buy anything they're sold if it's got hate and
fear in its heart. And Elizabeth will smile and welcome that
world in.

MARION *has stopped helping with the balloons.*

ELSIE. As I said, that's up for her to decide.

MARION *can't hide her frustration.*

Speak to Elizabeth about it if you feel so strongly. Phone her.

MARION. I'm not going to do that.

ELSIE. The two of you never shied away when it was your
mother or my phone bill.

MARION. Things change.

ELSIE. You two were inseparable.

MARION. Were.

ELSIE. You both live in London.

MARION. Not the same London.

ELSIE. A phone call, Elizabeth would appreciate a phone call.

MARION. No, she wouldn't.

ELSIE. Oh, she would. It wasn't that long ago you followed
her there.

MARION. I didn't follow her. It was my own choice. It had
nothing to do with Elizabeth.

A moment.

ELSIE. I had hoped for more than one child. It didn't happen.
But I always believed Elizabeth wouldn't suffer because you
had each other. Call her.

MARION. I don't think you know your daughter any more.

A moment. MARION *realises she has overstepped.*
MARION *goes back to blowing up a balloon.*

Shall I put the other balloons out?

ELSIE. Two per table.

MARION *starts to position the helium balloons. The*
atmosphere is still awkward.

MARION. These will look nice.

ELSIE *nods.*

The kids they'll all be gulping it down, won't they. The
helium. Funny voices.

ELSIE *nods. It's still awkward.* MARION *takes a breath*
of helium.

Are you expecting a large turnout tomorrow?

ELSIE. I wouldn't know.

MARION. Will you be ticking people's names off the list?

ELSIE. No, no, I just look after the hall.

The helium has run out.

MARION. You'd be able to tick names off just by the sight of
them.

ELSIE. Quite possibly.

MARION. Although there's a few new faces in and around,
aren't there?

ELSIE. A few.

MARION. Margaret Emery's old house, the people in there,
they're new, yes.

ELSIE. They are.

MARION. Are they nice?

ELSIE. I haven't really spoken to them, just a hello. He drives
somewhere for work. A long way, I'm told. An accountant.

MARION. He'll be voting then.

ELSIE. Maybe.

MARION. I can't.

ELSIE. No?

MARION. Because I'm here, aren't I. Not registered. And I didn't have time to set up a postal vote.

ELSIE. That's a shame.

MARION. Shame?

ELSIE. It seems important to you.

MARION. It's more than a shame. It's… What about you?

ELSIE. I don't really get involved in that.

MARION. Politics?

ELSIE. It's not for the likes of me.

MARION. You moved from a city to here, that's a very political decision.

ELSIE. I met a man and I didn't want to leave, I don't think politics has much to do with that.

MARION. Politics is a dirty word round here, isn't it.

ELSIE. I'm sure there are a lot dirtier.

MARION. Elsie, if you go through most towns all you see are boards up, here you wouldn't think there was a General Election taking place tomorrow.

ELSIE. Sam Robinson's expecting balloons to play with.

MARION. This is important.

ELSIE. I don't see you for half a year and the first time I do you shout at me about politics.

MARION. I'm not shouting. You're just not listening.

ELSIE. What's going on in your head, young lady?

MARION. A lot is going on if you must know. A lot.

ELSIE. I can see that.

MARION *blows up another balloon.*

Are you going to leave it at that? Stop blowing that and talk to me.

MARION. Sam Robinson is expecting balloons!

ELSIE. Put that down and talk to me.

A moment.

MARION. I drove through Newton yesterday.

ELSIE. Heatherview, you mean.

MARION. It's not been called that for a long time. It just keeps growing and growing.

ELSIE. Yes, it does.

MARION. Two hundred new homes on the old army base.

ELSIE. It's a nonsense.

MARION. People need houses, Elsie.

ELSIE. Not on a flood plain. It floods every time there's a drop of rain, pouring tarmac over it means it will be lifeboats floating by not lorries soon.

MARION. It won't affect you.

ELSIE. It will.

MARION. It's seven miles away!

ELSIE. I can hear lorries from our house now.

MARION. You're a long way from the road.

ELSIE. You've grown used to noise, that's your problem. Cities are full of noise.

No space for your own thoughts. I can hear a sparrow land.

MARION. No, you can't.

ELSIE. Not with all these lorries thundering by, feeding that town.

MARION. There's a Sainsbury's being built.

ELSIE. What does that mean?

MARION. It's a supermarket.

ELSIE. I know what it is.

MARION. You can buy pineapples there.

ELSIE. Why are you talking about pineapples?

MARION. It was an example.

ELSIE. I thought you were meant to be a punk, or something of the sort, and you're stood there praising Sainsbury's.

MARION. It's good for the area.

ELSIE. You know that the butcher's, the Christies' shop, will close down because of Sainsbury's. Why are you smiling, it's not funny.

MARION. And you say, politics isn't for you.

ELSIE. Yes, very good, you made a point.

MARION. On your doorstep suddenly it's everything. That place, that town, it's the future. Where people are going to end up.

ELSIE. I don't think that's true, darling.

MARION. In those boxed houses. A city that's a not a city, a village that's not a village.

ELSIE. Is this about your mother?

MARION. What's this got to do with Mum? I'm on about here, this place. The way you all romanticise it, as if it's better than places like Newton. It's not. I mean who actually works here? Yes, you and Stanley, but for how long? When I was young it was obvious. People actually looked like they worked on the land, were needed to work on the land, but now machines do that and because people can drive and commute to further than they ever did. It's a lifestyle here, not a living. So that traffic you hear, if you can hear traffic, is mostly those people who live in the village whose children Stanley teaches. This place!

ELSIE. You had a lovely life here.

MARION. Just because you can see roses doesn't mean everything smells like them.

ELSIE. Do you not remember the adventures you had?

MARION. I was a child, children have adventures in cardboard boxes. This place is too small.

ELSIE. Sometimes small is what people crave. Sometimes it's more than enough.

MARION. It's not though. It's dangerous.

ELSIE. Stanley obviously wasn't that good a teacher if you think that is what dangerous means.

MARION. How long does it take for a doctor to get out here?

ELSIE. Dr Harris lives in the village.

MARION. He's not that sort of doctor and you know it. John Ashton delivered me.

ELSIE. And you'll meet none healthier.

MARION. John Ashton is a bloody farmer!

ELSIE. That was twenty-seven years ago.

MARION. It's dangerous!

ELSIE. Dangerous! Ask anyone who lived through the war what danger was.

MARION. Here we go.

ELSIE. Ask Stanley. Ask him when he comes down later.

MARION. I'm not going to do that.

ELSIE. You've lived through nothing, darling.

MARION. Ah! It's become a competition for your generation – none of us can ever know what danger was because bombs didn't fall on our heads, as if that's the only form danger can take! Hold us all to ransom and whenever we complain, you didn't live through what we did. Well, no, but you don't live through what I do. Uncertainty. Nothing more dangerous than uncertainty. I wish we had a war, a common aim. Instead I've spent the last few years of my life watching bin bags piling up on every street corner. And people learning to hate each other and –

MARION *bursts one of the balloons.* MARION *sits down.* ELSIE *watches her. Eventually…*

You need to come with me to Newton later. Heatherview.

ELSIE. Why?

MARION. I want you to see something.

ELSIE. We don't need to see anything there.

MARION. Mum's going to need care.

ELSIE. No, no, no –

MARION. She will, Elsie.

ELSIE. Which she gets.

MARION. Professional. In the long term –

ELSIE. You want to put her in a home?

MARION. Not a home. It's purpose built.

ELSIE. Are you serious?

MARION. If she sells the house, she could live there comfortably. It has people on site.

ELSIE. What people?

MARION. A warden. Others.

ELSIE. Strangers. She'll be left looking every day out of a window at a place she doesn't know.

MARION. Nobody wants this to be the solution.

ELSIE. It's only you that's talking in this way.

MARION. And you'll take care of her, will you?

ELSIE. Of course I will! For over thirty years we've not gone a day without looking after each other. And so will others. This is her home. Your mother was born here. In her house. There's a path that she's worn between here and the village.

MARION. You mean to The Plough from collecting my dad.

ELSIE. Remember when he died how the village was there for your mother? It will be the same again today, tomorrow and every day she lives here. To take that away when she needs it most.

MARION. Do you know what her window overlooks? It overlooks a field. It overlooks a brook. It overlooks trees of all sorts of variety, with names I should know but don't. It overlooks places where birds perch and foxes shit and a myriad of other life. It overlooks a lot of beautiful things.

ELSIE. Her life.

MARION. Do you know what it doesn't overlook? It doesn't overlook a road. It doesn't overlook a doctor's, it doesn't overlook any of the things that she's going to need as her condition gets worse and worse.

ELSIE. You don't see it, do you.

MARION. See what?

ELSIE. You never felt it. That's fine. You wanted out, that's fine. Here wasn't enough for you, for Elizabeth, and I accept that. But do show it some respect, as for me, for your mother, there's everything. Let this village do what it does – let it look after her.

MARION. Can't ask that of people.

ELSIE. It's not an ask. It's what people do here.

A moment.

Look at the board.

MARION. It's the bridge results, I know what it is.

ELSIE. Go over and look.

MARION *does*.

Do you recognise any names?

MARION. …Mum…

ELSIE. Every week she's here.

MARION. She's bottom of the league.

ELSIE. I never said she was any good. The other notice. To your left.

MARION. WI minutes?

ELSIE. Look who had any other business.

MARION....Mum...

ELSIE. Every week it's the same. Always chipping in, the bench by the bus stop needs re-staining, the lamp in the village green needs a new bulb, a wasp has been making the phone box its home – your mother will find anything to add to any other business.

MARION *looks round.*

It's these things, these people, that get her out of bed. That help her.

MARION *looks round the hall, memories from her past suddenly become clearer.*

MARION. Do you miss Elizabeth?

ELSIE. She's my daughter.

MARION. She's never coming back here, is she.

ELSIE. No.

MARION. I did follow her. Must have looked so pathetic.

ELSIE. It was the right thing for you to do.

MARION. It wasn't.

ELSIE. You hated the quiet.

MARION. When?

ELSIE. When you were a baby, we used to have play records just to get you to sleep.

MARION. I used to soil myself six times a day as well as a baby, I've grown out of things since then! I tried to be like Elizabeth. The suits. The talk. The confidence. I thought I could change, I couldn't – I just didn't expect her to keep changing too.

ELSIE. Elizabeth has always been driven.

MARION. I was older but I was always looking up at her.
I never could keep up. Don't have the same genes, do I.

ELSIE. Your mother did a good job with you.

MARION. Well, that cancelled out the job Dad did.

A moment.

ELSIE. Do you know when the last time I went to London was?

MARION. No.

ELSIE. You would have been about six. I took your mother.

MARION. Mum? She never told me she'd been.

ELSIE. Well, she has. Stanley looked after you both. There was
no train from Heatherview back then. We took a bus then a
bus then another. We didn't do too much when we got there.
We walked the streets. Looked in windows. It was more than
I remembered and less than your mother dreamed it would be.

MARION. Why did she never tell me she'd been?

ELSIE. It's hard being a parent. Ever so hard. It's up to your
children to discover what they think of a place. Even if it
means that as parents we have to say goodbye.

MARION. I've failed.

ELSIE. You've done no such thing.

MARION. I have. There's no job. It's not good there. My flat is
riddled with mould. I'm not a punk. I dress like one because
it's as far from what I thought Elizabeth is and I thought that
might be how I might make it work, but I don't even like my
hair. Or Blondie.

ELSIE. I'm not saying come back. I'm not saying this is the
answer. All I'll tell you is it's not a failure.

MARION *looks around the room.*

MARION. I was sick in that corner. Elizabeth's tenth birthday.

ELSIE. I remember.

MARION. You do?

ELSIE. Who do you think cleaned it up?

MARION. We'd been running around like crazy. Cake high. Music blaring.

ELSIE. I remember.

MARION. I was at my happiest when I was running around in my socks sliding about. I could almost do half the room.

ELSIE. I know you could.

MARION. Even Elizabeth couldn't do more than that. That was fun.

ELSIE *goes to the record player. She plays a song.*

ELSIE. Give it a go.

MARION. I'm not going to run about in my socks.

ELSIE. Why not?

MARION. I'm twenty-six years old.

ELSIE. And?

MARION *can't find an answer.*

When your mother was your age she would have danced till her feet gave way on that very spot. Even with you tucked under her arm it wouldn't stop her. Your life's not a Lowry painting, darling. Allow yourself a little moment of enjoyment.

MARION *takes her shoes off and walks into the middle of the room, she then tentatively starts to slide along the floor, the enjoyment building and building until* MARION *collapses on the floor and starts to laugh, a sad laugh.* ELSIE *waits until* MARION *is calm and then helps* MARION *to her feet, they hug. Eventually they let go.*

We have a little boy arriving soon who needs to have the best day of his life.

MARION. You know it won't always be parties that fill this room. It will be goodbyes, memorials, those events that everyone wants to forget.

ELSIE. Well, that's one problem solved – you should become a goth, not a punk.

A moment.

People grow up. People get older. People get weaker. But let them do it on their terms. Marion? On their terms.

MARION. Is that what you'd want? To stay?

ELSIE. This is my home.

MARION. But it's only that now because you've still got people, you can still do things – what about when that goes?

ELSIE *doesn't answer.*

I have to go and see Mum. Elsie, please think about what I've said. Nobody wants to be the last one standing at the party.

A moment. MARION *goes.*

ELSIE. Darling, it's only in the silence you realise how good a time you had.

ELSIE *takes in the hall. For a second the silence is deafening. She shakes the feeling off and goes back to setting up for the party.*

1998

*9th July 1998. Morning. The start of a muggy day. The village
hall is set up for a function. A table is laid in preparation for a
buffet, chairs are neatly arranged, etc. ELSIE, now seventy-two,
enters. ELSIE has a heavy coat on, underneath she is all
dressed in black, she has a bag with her. ELSIE takes in the
room, allows its history, its memories, to wash over her.
Perhaps ELSIE smiles, rubs her hand over the tablecloth, there
is no rush. From within the bag, ELSIE takes out a framed
photo – it is of a handsome man, in his RAF uniform. She
eventually puts it on the table. ELSIE takes out another photo,
it is of her wedding day. SCARLETT enters the hall, an energy
alien to the environment.*

SCARLETT. Gosh, this is so completely charming, in a rustic
way. Obviously, it's been a while since a little love was
showered upon it. Still it feels sooo welcoming. Hello.
HELLO.

ELSIE. I can hear you.

SCARLETT. I was saying it's obviously been a while since this
building was given a little love.

ELSIE. I'm not deaf, I could hear you. You're early.

SCARLETT. The early bird catches the worm.

ELSIE. Best off putting them in the fridge.

SCARLETT. Putting what in what fridge?

ELSIE. The sandwiches.

SCARLETT. Erm, what sandwiches?

ELSIE turns and faces SCARLETT for the first time.

ELSIE. You're not her, are you.

SCARLETT. Who is her? She sounds wonderfully vague.

ELSIE. The girl bringing the sandwiches. I've forgotten her name…

SCARLETT. The sandwich girl.

ELSIE. Yes.

SCARLETT. Oh, that is hilarious. Don't tell me this girl was making them as well.

ELSIE. She was.

SCARLETT. Jeremy is going to absolutely howl at this.

ELSIE. Jeremy?

SCARLETT. My husband. Me, making sandwiches, I can't even toast, toast!! I've been mistaken for a florist once, that was hilarious as I'm utterly hopeless with flowers, they always end up completely dead in my hands. I let Jeremy take care of the garden, it's much more his area of speciality.

ELSIE. Is it?

SCARLETT. Yes, oh god yes. Jeremy is much more familiar with that world. Nature. I really am so taken aback – from the outside it looks so ramshackle, but once you're in here, it's got a certain character. What is this made of, is it wood?

ELSIE. Yes, it's wood.

SCARLETT. Oh, how utterly kitsch. I can smell the history, or perhaps that's actually mould. The curtains do look slightly on the wain.

ELSIE. Who are you?

SCARLETT. Scarlett.

ELSIE. Scarlett?

SCARLETT. Yes, from next door.

ELSIE. The big house?

SCARLETT. Oh, is that what people call it? Hilarious.

ELSIE. Woodside House?

SCARLETT. Do not let Jeremy hear you say 'house', he'll have a complete hissy fit. He's always dreamt of owning a home with the word 'hall' in it, you see. So that's what we're calling it now.

ELSIE. Woodside Hall?

SCARLETT. Exactly!

ELSIE. So that's you next door then, is it.

SCARLETT. Guilty.

ELSIE. I've been wondering who you'd be.

SCARLETT. Here I am.

ELSIE. I've not seen you before.

SCARLETT. We've not been here for long at all, a matter of months, furniture is very much still in transit, or being sourced to fill the extra space. Oh, aren't you good, that is seamless.

ELSIE. Seamless?

SCARLETT. The talk of furniture. The chairs. They will be so perfect.

ELSIE. Perfect?

SCARLETT. Absolutely perfect. Such an absolute lifesaver. Am I take to them now?

ELSIE. The chairs?

SCARLETT. I had assumed somebody would be here to assist. Not to be rude, I am sure you're very strong, but I can't see you hulking them up the drive.

ELSIE. You can't take the chairs.

SCARLETT. Me, no. I could take one perhaps, but not so many. And I don't have the time to be hauling them back and forth. No, god no. I've got so much more to be doing.

ELSIE. You can't take the chairs.

SCARLETT. I'm sorry, what?

ELSIE. Who told you you could take the chairs?

SCARLETT. Was it not you?

ELSIE. I have no business talking about chairs to anyone.

SCARLETT. Oh my god, are you not Claire?

ELSIE. Claire?

SCARLETT. Claire... Emery...?

ELSIE. No, I'm not Claire Emery.

SCARLETT. Oh, well, there we go, that makes so much more
    sense. Claire and I we only spoke on the phone you see, and
    I thought you might have forgotten – a little memory lapse!
    Nothing wrong with that, it happens to everyone with age!
    But no, no you're fully compos mentis and it's me that has
    been the bull in the china shop!

ELSIE. Claire Emery is half my age.

SCARLETT. Really?

ELSIE. Her mother, Margaret, was my age.

SCARLETT. It must be the accent, I'm still acclimatising
    myself to it. My radar is way, way off. I can't calculate any
    ages, or sometimes gender, local four-year-old girls could be
    seventy-year-old men to my ear! I'll adapt, with time, I'm
    sure. Maybe I'll even end up joining the club!

ELSIE. Claire Emery sounds nothing like me.

SCARLETT. Oh, trust me, she does.

ELSIE. Claire said you could take the chairs?

SCARLETT. Twenty chairs we agreed upon.

ELSIE. For today?

SCARLETT. She said pop over on Friday and we can sort
    you out.

ELSIE. Today's Thursday.

SCARLETT. Oh I know, but I saw you come in and I thought
    why not strike whilst the iron's hot. It would save me so such
    stress tomorrow, if I could be ahead of the curve.

ELSIE. The curve?

SCARLETT. Oh yes, I've got so much prep to do for the party. Thirty years old on Saturday! Would you believe it! Where did the time go? And all the world and his wives are descending on Saturday. And presently, in the guest-to-chair ratio we are severely lacking, which I am sure you can appreciate would be a complete disaster.

ELSIE. You can't take the chairs now. Today is Thursday.

SCARLETT. I know it's Thursday.

ELSIE. They're needed for today.

SCARLETT. It would be such a help though –

ELSIE. No.

SCARLETT. I beg your pardon?

ELSIE. Your ears work fine. Whatever arrangement you've come to with Claire, that's for tomorrow. So come back then for the chairs.

SCARLETT. What's your name?

ELSIE. Elsie.

SCARLETT. Well, I must say, Elsie, this is going very much against what I was told that the countryside was all about. Community spirit, looking out for your neighbours.

ELSIE. You can't have the chairs as people will need to sit on them.

SCARLETT. What people?

ELSIE. The people who are coming here.

SCARLETT. For what?

ELSIE. You can't have the chairs, we've covered that.

SCARLETT. I'm asking a very simple question. I'm planning ahead, if there are going to be lots of cars spilling out of the car park and lining the road, I'll have to warn the delivery company that it will be harder to negotiate.

ELSIE. It's a memorial.

SCARLETT. Oh god, for someone who's died?

ELSIE. That's what memorials are for, yes.

SCARLETT. Don't people normally have them in pubs or such places?

ELSIE. People have them where they want.

SCARLETT. Bit bleak. I thought we were going to be living next door to the bridge club, or the Christmas panto, not memorial services.

ELSIE. Perhaps it's full of memories.

SCARLETT. I suppose people have attachments to all sorts of places. So you're here to set it up, are you?

ELSIE. That's right.

SCARLETT. Is that why you're wearing black?

ELSIE. That's right.

SCARLETT. Whilst everyone else is at the church?

ELSIE. Nobody's at the church.

SCARLETT. No?

ELSIE. The service is at twelve.

SCARLETT *picks up one of the pictures.*

SCARLETT. Is this him?

ELSIE. Shouldn't touch things.

SCARLETT. Handsome man.

ELSIE. Yes.

SCARLETT. Uh-oh watch out, man in uniform.

ELSIE. The Air Force.

SCARLETT. A pilot?!

ELSIE. That's right, yes.

SCARLETT. I love holidays. What's his name?

ELSIE. Stanley.

SCARLETT. Stanley. Was he from here? From Woodside?

ELSIE. He was, yes.

SCARLETT. How old was he?

ELSIE. Seventy-two.

SCARLETT. That's a good innings.

ELSIE. Always want a bit longer.

SCARLETT. Did you know him well?

ELSIE. Yes, I did.

SCARLETT. Nice man?

ELSIE. I'd say so.

SCARLETT. What makes a man nice out here?

ELSIE. Same as most places. Not being a self-centered arse.

SCARLETT. I totally agree. I hate those sorts of people.
    Expecting many?

ELSIE. He was a popular man. Headmaster at the school for
    over thirty years, so I would expect so. The girl who was
    making the sandwiches, she was somebody he taught.

SCARLETT. The one who you got me confused with?

ELSIE. That's right.

SCARLETT. Hilarious, I didn't go to school here.

ELSIE. That's pretty obvious to me now.

SCARLETT. Is that his wife?

ELSIE. What?

SCARLETT. The photo you're holding?

ELSIE. It is, yes.

    SCARLETT *holds her hand out*. ELSIE *hands over the
    photo*. SCARLETT *studies it*.

SCARLETT. Elsie, this looks a lot like a much younger version
    of you.

ELSIE. That would make sense.

SCARLETT. Oh my god, Elsie, is Stanley your husband? I mean, was he your husband, I'm terrible with bloody tenses sometimes. Elsie?

ELSIE. Yes, he was my husband.

SCARLETT. Oh god, Elsie, I feel terrible. Utterly terrible, trying to steal the chairs of your mourners. I would think that I was a monster if I was you.

ELSIE. Then I'll let you think that.

SCARLETT. Can I offer you an apology?

ELSIE. You can.

SCARLETT. And would you accept it?

ELSIE. I've got a lot of setting up to be doing.

SCARLETT. There were no signs, Elsie.

ELSIE. I thought it would be pretty obvious myself.

A moment.

SCARLETT. You shouldn't be alone right now. Where's your family? Where are your friends? Why aren't they helping you? Why are you here by yourself?

ELSIE. Because I wanted to be.

SCARLETT. Surely not.

ELSIE. You should get back to the 'Hall'.

SCARLETT. How can I after what you've just told me?

ELSIE. By walking.

SCARLETT. You should be helped.

ELSIE. Do you think nobody's offered? I had to tell half the village not to come.

SCARLETT. Well, they may think they're helping but they're not. I remember Mum trying to do everything by herself when Daddy went – it was not healthy. In the end she crumbled. So I'm here for you now.

ELSIE. When you came in five minutes ago you were too busy to move chairs.

SCARLETT. This is what being part of a village is about. The helping. The community –

ELSIE. Let me be, will you.

SCARLETT. Elsie –

ELSIE. I want to be by myself.

ELSIE *takes the photo from* SCARLETT *and puts it back on the table.* ELSIE *now has her back to* SCARLETT. SCARLETT *waits awkwardly, suddenly a fish out of water.*

SCARLETT. I'm terribly sorry for your loss. Elsie, I'm terribly sorry.

ELSIE. Well, you got there in the end, didn't you.

SCARLETT. I am though. Terribly. I truly am, I know all about loss.

ELSIE. So you've said.

SCARLETT. I'm only next door if you ever, ever, ever, ever, I mean ever need anything.

SCARLETT *goes.* ELSIE *goes back to putting out more photographs.* SCARLETT, *who has been hovering in the entrance, returns.*

Elsie?

ELSIE *waits in silence, hoping* SCARLETT *goes.*

Elsie. This is not the way I hoped to meet people.

ELSIE *continues to ignore* SCARLETT.

Can I not help in any conceivable way? It's terribly muggy, I could open the windows. You must admit fresh air is required in here.

ELSIE. That smell will take more than a few open windows to get rid of.

SCARLETT. This is all new to me. These surroundings. I don't necessarily know the best way to fit in.

ELSIE. Well, now you know how not to.

SCARLETT. That seems rather fair. If you have any advice on how to go about things better – I'm all ears.

ELSIE. Listening to people's wishes would be a –

SCARLETT. Yes, listening, but I honestly, if you don't mind me saying, think that you shouldn't be by yourself right now.

ELSIE. Tell me your name again.

SCARLETT. Scarlett.

ELSIE. Scarlett, I'll give you some advice.

SCARLETT. Oh please, thank you.

ELSIE. Get some curtains for your bathroom.

SCARLETT. Curtains?

ELSIE. In your bathroom.

SCARLETT. That's not what I was expecting.

ELSIE. Otherwise you risk becoming a local attraction.

SCARLETT. I don't follow.

ELSIE. The owner before those you bought the big house off. She was a woman like yourself. Round the back of the Hall, if you jump over the brook, you can see through into your garden. The bathroom overlooks the garden. If you could never find a teenage boy at dinnertime you knew where to go. From three villages over they'd come. Huddled together in the hedges.

SCARLETT. No!

ELSIE. Oh yes, it was a rite of passage, her showers.

SCARLETT. You mean, they were in the hedges, communally…

ELSIE. There're lots of nutrients in the soil there, let's leave it at that. So there you go, that's my advice to you.

SCARLETT. Well, that's another thing to add to the Hall's to-do list then. It really needs a bit of a facelift. Brought into the future. Presently it's very authentic.

ELSIE. Authentic?

SCARLETT. You know you're in the countryside.

ELSIE. You are in the countryside.

SCARLETT. I know and it really doesn't hide it. My friends are amazed I have an Aga.

They call me the Lady of the Manor. Sing 'Country House' to me down the phone. I don't actually know how the Aga works but they don't need to know that.

ELSIE. You're not going to let me be, are you?

SCARLETT. Elsie, my mum was so pig-headed with Daddy. She thought she was being strong for me and my brother by not involving us. Not involving us. It set her back in the long run.

ELSIE. At my age, death is not such a surprise. I've lost neighbours, siblings, parents, closest, most dearest friends.

SCARLETT. It's different with it being your husband though.

ELSIE. Countryside is new to you, isn't it.

SCARLETT. Is it that obvious? Is it the shoes? Jeremy keeps trying to get me to wear wellies but I thought that was just playing into the stereotype.

ELSIE. It's not the shoes.

SCARLETT. It's not about saying how heavy the chairs are, is it? As I know country women are hearty, but I've not skipped a day of Elle Macpherson's body workout regime in months, so I think I can hold my own when it comes to lifting –

ELSIE. I've heard more words from you in ten minutes than I ever heard from my husband.

SCARLETT. Quiet, was he?

ELSIE. I didn't think so at the time.

ELSIE *sighs, she stares directly at* SCARLETT – *she can't help but smile.*

SCARLETT. What?

ELSIE. I'm scared you remind me of someone.

SCARLETT. Who?

A moment.

Who? Oh go on, tell me. Is it Posh Spice? Please say it's not Posh Spice.

ELSIE. There are some flowers over there that need to go in the vases, if you won't go then at least be of some use.

SCARLETT. You trust me with flowers?

ELSIE. You'll just be putting them in a vase, I hardly need you to be Capability Brown. Go on then. Water's in the kitchen. Then one vase per table.

SCARLETT goes to the kitchen. ELSIE takes a moment. SCARLETT comes back with a jug of water.

SCARLETT. The water goes in the vases?

ELSIE. It'll do the flowers more good there than on the floor.

A moment.

SCARLETT. I don't know what I'm doing.

ELSIE. Oh, pull yourself together. Pour it and then add flowers till it looks pretty. Prove Jeremy wrong.

SCARLETT starts to arrange the flowers.

SCARLETT. How long were you married?

ELSIE. A long time.

SCARLETT. My friend Grace was married for two years, she called that a long time.

ELSIE. Fifty-one years.

SCARLETT. Fifty-one years? Oh my god, that's for ever. You don't look old enough.

ELSIE. Yes, I do. I was twenty-one, he was twenty-two, when we got married.

SCARLETT. And you were together all that time?

ELSIE. Yes.

SCARLETT. Continuously, never any, well, how is the polite way to /

ELSIE. You don't need to ask.

SCARLETT. /say it, gaps, gaps I think is the best w–

ELSIE. No.

SCARLETT. Amazing. That's amazing. I've only been married three years and it feels like an eternity.

ELSIE. We met here.

SCARLETT. *Here*, here?

ELSIE. That's right.

SCARLETT. At a memorial?

ELSIE. No. There was a welcome-home party for those who made it back from the war. Stanley was one of those lucky ones. Our first dance, our first kiss, our wedding reception, our fiftieth-anniversary party –

SCARLETT. Oh my god, that would have only been… last year!

ELSIE. Yes. A lot has happened under this roof. It didn't used to look this tired. 'Retro'. We're hoping for some Lottery funding. Give it a millennium makeover.

SCARLETT. Oh, I dream of that, a lovely Lottery win.

ELSIE. I think some would say you've already won that.

SCARLETT. Me?

ELSIE. Yes. It's a rather large shadow your house casts over this village.

SCARLETT. Is it, I thought we were south-facing? I wish I'd seen you both. It's such a simple dress.

ELSIE. As was the day. As simple as you could imagine. We swayed together to music you'd call old-fashioned.

SCARLETT. (Bros?)

ELSIE. It rained but we didn't care. We had our friends. We had each other. It was our day.

SCARLETT. Jeremy and I got married at his golf club, I don't think they cover and cater for all stages of a couple's life there. Not that we'd want to go back, we had to fight so hard to get the liver pâté, I couldn't face that again. Am I doing this right?

ELSIE. I've not got any medals to give out.

SCARLETT. But if you did?

ELSIE. Keep going as you are.

SCARLETT. Have you always lived in Woodside?

ELSIE. Me and Stanley, yes. We got married. We moved into his parents' house. They died not long after. So we never moved out. That's the only place Stanley ever lived. Aside from three years when he was at war.

SCARLETT. So he got to see some of the world, travel.

ELSIE. Not quite what Thomas Cook would advertise as travelling.

SCARLETT. I can't imagine being in one place all my life.

ELSIE. There used to be a lot of others like that here. Stanley is – was, one of the last though.

SCARLETT. A dying breed. Oh god, what am I saying. Complete foot in mouth. How long is it since Stanley... you know...

ELSIE. Died? You can say it, I know Stanley's dead. I'm not expecting him to walk out of his shed at any point. A week.

SCARLETT. Was it a surprise?

ELSIE. It wasn't a very good one if it was.

A moment.

Stanley's heart just stopped. He'd been watching England versus Argentina in the World Cup. He said something rude about David Beckham and then went outside to feed the birds. I found Stanley by the bird table. He still had the seeds in his hand. Not one was spilt. I don't know how long he'd been there.

SCARLETT. God, I hate football at the best of times, what with this bloody World Cup on every channel right now, and now I know it played a part in Stanley dying –

ELSIE. It was a coronary failure. It could have happened at any moment.

SCARLETT. You're ever so calm. I would be in tears at the very mention of Jeremy, if he'd died.

ELSIE. Crying won't bring him back, darling.

SCARLETT. I find crying cathartic. I spent all of yesterday in the back garden, looking out over the fields, up at the sky, the colours, all alone, and I just wept and wept. It actually hurt after a while. By the time Jeremy came back, I was so completely exhausted, he found me fast asleep on the grass.

ELSIE. Dr Diprose will be coming to pay her respects later, perhaps you should pop by and have a word.

SCARLETT. You mean I'm invited?

ELSIE. It's not a black-tie ball, darling. You can come if you really want to.

SCARLETT. That is so unbelievably kind of you. My first village invite! Do I bring a bottle?

ELSIE. No.

SCARLETT. I'm really touched.

ELSIE. I didn't grow up here, you know.

SCARLETT. No?

ELSIE. I came here at nineteen. I did the same move as you.

SCARLETT. London? Are you telling me I'm a modern-day version of you!

ELSIE. I wouldn't quite say that, I came because of the war.

SCARLETT. Still though, you know what that world is like. The glamour, the fashion, the restaurants –

ELSIE. It wasn't glitz and glamour, my version.

SCARLETT. I suppose that was a long, long, long time ago. Things do change, Elsie. Especially in the cities. I feel like, coming here, I've stepped back into the Victorian times.

ELSIE. Oh, Stanley would have laughed at that.

SCARLETT. At what?

ELSIE. Bless you, darling. Here you noticed when a window frame's painted different, when cars no longer just take up a driveway but the pavement too. Change doesn't creep up on you here, it announces itself very loudly.

SCARLETT. Oh god, I must be totally like an earthquake in that case. Are people going to hate me? I don't want to be hated.

ELSIE. Plenty of people hated me when I arrived.

SCARLETT. Who could hate you?

ELSIE. Well, only really Mary Swan hated me. I stole Stanley from her, you see.

SCARLETT. You stole Stanley? Look at you go.

ELSIE. I didn't actually steal him.

SCARLETT. She was with Stanley?

ELSIE. Only in Mary's head. But that didn't stop her hating me. It took Mary Swan thirty-odd years to actually say something nice to me and that was only because my goddaughter, Marion, ended up marrying her son.

SCARLETT. That's lovely that you're now friends but I don't have anyone that I can pimp out should I become a figure of hate.

ELSIE. Scarlett, the people who sold the Hall to you, they didn't mix with the village. The big house was just a toy to them, they came as and when. Put nothing into the village.

SCARLETT. Oh, that's not what I want to be like! I want to be part of the village.

ELSIE. Well, that's a good start. Why have you moved here?

SCARLETT. You sound puzzled.

ELSIE. There are plenty of big houses elsewhere.

SCARLETT. It's a nice village.

ELSIE. You think so? You barely know it.

SCARLETT. Well, you've lived here for over fifty years. That's a pretty good indicator.

ELSIE. When I moved here all I had was women my age to talk to. The village has got older and older. The shop has gone. It's not the same.

SCARLETT. Would you not move here again if you could?

ELSIE. I don't know if I would move here today.

A moment.

SCARLETT. Jeremy grew up in the country. He spoke so warmly of his childhood. Of every day being an adventure. I grew up in a place that was quite forgettable. The suburbs. Of not even a city, of a town. I know you wouldn't think that if you met me now. That's what seven years of London does to you. And so, Jeremy kept telling me that I was stressed, because the hours I was working were unbelievably intense, and every day for the last two years we've talked about starting a family and Jeremy thought that this would be the best way to give us that chance, for me to destress, help with the conception process and so we found the Hall and now I don't have to worry about work and we can concentrate solely on making the children, but the thing is that's all well and good but you then actually have to spend time together in order for any chance of conception to actually happen. I can't just magic his beans inside me.

ELSIE. No, I don't suppose you can.

SCARLETT. On Saturday people will come to my party and tell me how jealous they are. They'll say what a wonderful view. And they're right, it is. It is what a painter would paint, and if I looked at that painting in a gallery I'd say that is a wonderful view. But actually living in it, I don't see that – all I see is nothing. I see an empty space. Jeremy is so convinced this is the right place for a child… I don't know…

ELSIE. Maybe it will be, maybe it won't be.

SCARLETT. Was it for you and Stanley?

ELSIE. We thought it was. Our daughter, Elizabeth, wasn't as certain. Elizabeth left here almost the day she could.

SCARLETT. Why?

ELSIE. Because she wanted a different life.

SCARLETT. She wasn't happy here?

ELSIE. Not in the way she wanted.

SCARLETT. And she's happy now? Obviously not right now with her dad having died.

ELSIE. She's happy. Elizabeth lives in America now. New York. She works in banking. As far from this as you could ever dream.

SCARLETT. I love New York! You must have loved visiting her.

ELSIE. We never went.

SCARLETT. No way! I've been at least three times. *When Harry Met Sally* is my all time favourite film, every time we go I make sure we go to Katz's Deli so I can re-enact the orgasm scene. Jeremy pretends to be mortified but he secretly loves it.

ELSIE. I've never seen the film.

SCARLETT. Well, we will rectify that! It's not just about a woman faking an orgasm in a restaurant, it's about the beauty and magic of love and what it is to find...

ELSIE. What?

SCARLETT. ...a soulmate...

ELSIE. Films have been made about much worse things.

SCARLETT *picks up a picture of Stanley and Marion, from Marion's wedding day.*

SCARLETT. Is this Elizabeth?

ELSIE. No, Elizabeth has never got married. That's Marion. She's my closest friend, Dot's, daughter. Stanley walked Marion down the aisle.

SCARLETT. Oh, so these children aren't your grandchildren?

ELSIE. No. Elizabeth doesn't have any children. Those are
    Marion and Ben's children. It's not a photo collection of
    a random assortment of children.

SCARLETT. That is a lot less weird.

ELSIE. That's Emily, Marion and Ben's youngest, she's thirteen
    now. And that's Scott, he's sixteen. And that's Sam, he's
    Marion's stepson, he'll be twenty-four or twenty-five now.
    They all live up in Aberdeen.

SCARLETT. At least that's a little closer than New York!

ELSIE. A little, yes. Marion's a primary-school teacher. Stanley
    gave her her first job. Ben works out on the oil rigs. He does
    rope access work. He had been a tree surgeon round here, but
    the money for the same skills was too appealing.

SCARLETT. I always imagined boys would have a much better
    time in the countryside – all these trees to climb!

ELSIE. They all grow up loving climbing trees, it's only when
    they get older girls are told they shouldn't.

SCARLETT. Will they all be here later?

ELSIE. They will. Elizabeth is back for two weeks.

SCARLETT. From New York?

ELSIE. That's right. She's at the church sorting the flowers.
    Marion and Ben are getting the children ready for the
    service. They've only been to their grandmother's before and
    that was seven years ago, so they're rather inexperienced and
    sensitive when it comes to death.

    ELSIE *hands over a photo of her, Dorothy, Stanley, Marion
    and Elizabeth. They are outside in a garden. The children
    are seven at the time. It is full of joy.*

    That's Dot there in that one. Their grandmother.

SCARLETT. You wouldn't be able to tell her and Marion apart
    would you.

ELSIE. No, although Marion spent long enough trying to look
    different.

ELSIE *holds the photo. So precious. A golden moment somehow captured in time.*

SCARLETT. Oh my God, Elsie, is Dot who I reminded you of?! I am so flattered, your closest friend. I mean, wow! Although I would say that what she's wearing it's not really me. Colour-wise.

ELSIE *turns away from* SCARLETT. *Looks out of the window or at a noticeboard. A moment.*

Are the flowers all right like this?

ELSIE. They'll be fine.

SCARLETT. I can move them again if you like.

ELSIE. They'll be fine.

SCARLETT. It's no problem.

ELSIE. They'll be fine.

SCARLETT. There must be more that I can do.

ELSIE. Check the record player works.

SCARLETT. Do you mean the CD player, Elsie? Record players are even more ancient than this hall.

ELSIE. That.

SCARLETT. Yes, that's a CD player.

ELSIE. Marion put some of Stanley's favourite songs on to a disc.

SCARLETT. CD.

ELSIE. I don't really know what I'm doing with that.

SCARLETT *goes to the CD player.*

SCARLETT. The CD that's in?

ELSIE. Perhaps.

SCARLETT. Leave it with me.

She turns it on. A song starts.

Sound familiar?

ELSIE *nods.* SCARLETT *skips to the next track she does the same again and then again.*

ELSIE. Stop pressing the button.

SCARLETT. I was checking they all work.

ELSIE. Stop fiddling and let one play.

SCARLETT *nods and steps away. A beautiful song from a different time.* ELSIE *stops what she's doing. She listens. It's a song we may have heard before in 1953. It is the music that was playing when Stanley first asked* ELSIE *to dance.*

SCARLETT. Elsie?

ELSIE. We first danced to this song.

ELSIE *continues to listen.*

That'll do for now. We know it works.

SCARLETT *stops the CD player. Eventually...*

SCARLETT. Let me look at Stanley again. He was incredibly handsome, Elsie.

ELSIE. He was easy on the eye, yes.

SCARLETT. No wonder Mary wanted him for herself. I would have given you a run for your money if we were stood here all those years ago. What?

ELSIE. I'd have bit your pretty head off, darling.

SCARLETT. I bet you would.

A moment.

ELSIE. Ours was a quiet house. Some houses in this village you can hear from the other end. But not ours. We never argued. We never raised our voices. You can't hear smiles. That's what filled our house. Smiles. I'm not saying Stanley didn't used to wind me up something rotten at times. Toilet roll. Toilet roll! He'd leave the empty roll on the rail. You know when it has come to an end? Stanley wouldn't replace it with a fresh roll. He'd leave the sad little piece of cardboard on the holder. I'd always end up having to put in the bin, which was only five feet from the actual toilet.

SCARLETT. That is totally a male thing. Jeremy is guilty of that. So annoying.

ELSIE. It's the simplest of things.

SCARLETT. Just put it in the bin.

ELSIE. Otherwise he was the most tidy of men. But that. That toilet roll. No, never. I think Stanley enjoyed the game of it. And you know that was the last thing I asked him to do. That was the last thing I said to him. Make sure you put the toilet roll in the bin. Toilet roll! There are so many things I didn't get to say to him. So many things.

SCARLETT. He would have known.

ELSIE. So many things.

SCARLETT. He would have known.

SCARLETT takes ELSIE's hand.

He would have known.

A moment.

Did he put the toilet roll in the bin?

ELSIE. No, of course, he didn't.

A smile. A moment passes.

SCARLETT. Are you scared of being lonely?

ELSIE. There's not a moment when I won't miss him.

SCARLETT. Is it not true that if you've spent your life with someone, that when one goes, the other follows quickly?

ELSIE. He can wait a bit longer for me.

SCARLETT. I don't know, it happens all the time.

ELSIE. What with the war, life was given away very cheaply when I was young. When you know a lot of life has been lost so young you embrace every second, you do not wish it to end.

SCARLETT. We're so oblivious to all of that my generation. I wrote a letter of complaint to Waitrose about the shape of an avocado once. How will you fill your time?

ELSIE. We weren't joined at the hip. I'll find things or even more things if those things aren't enough.

SCARLETT. You could go on Saga holidays. They do trips for widows, well I'm certain they do. If not then they must start as what an absolute gold mine that group is. Amazing opportunity to meet a new man.

ELSIE. I won't be doing that.

SCARLETT. Mustn't rule it out.

ELSIE. I've been lucky enough to have enough love to fill many lifetimes.

SCARLETT. You should definitely travel, see the world. New York!

ELSIE. I've never been on a plane.

SCARLETT. You mean you've never been on holiday?

ELSIE. We've been on holidays.

SCARLETT. In a car? In this country? That doesn't count as a holiday.

ELSIE. Yes, it does.

SCARLETT. Really?

ELSIE. Yes. Flying wasn't really for Stanley, after the war he'd seen enough of the inside of planes.

SCARLETT. You have a chance now to try things for yourself.

ELSIE. He never stopped me doing anything.

SCARLETT. Perhaps he did – unintentionally. Are you sure this is even where you want to be?

ELSIE. It's our home.

SCARLETT. What I'm sort of trying to say it's got to be your home from now on.

ELSIE. You don't have to go far to see a lot, darling.

SCARLETT. But you do. That's just like a fact.

A moment.

Ignore me, I don't know what I'm talking about.

ELSIE. Perhaps you're right.

SCARLETT. No, no, no ignore me. According to the quiz I took in Jeremy's copy of *Loaded* I am a psychopath.

ELSIE *smiles. A moment.*

Is Stanley being buried?

ELSIE. Cremated. Then scattered somewhere special.

SCARLETT. What, in here?!

ELSIE. No.

SCARLETT. Going to say I know little about health and safety but I'm certain that even in the countryside that wouldn't be permitted.

ELSIE. He always wanted to be scattered in our garden. So that's what I'll do. In amongst his roses. And then when I go, I'll follow suit.

SCARLETT. Mum kept Daddy's ashes under the sink for ages. She didn't know what to do with him. Eventually we scattered them in the flower bed by the side of the kitchen. He used to sit there in the evening and smoke, totally blissfully unaware that that was what was actually killing him. Somebody else lives there now. Me and Jeremy drove past a couple of years ago. I wanted to show Jeremy where I grew up. New owners had extended the house. They put a conservatory over the top of where we'd scattered Daddy's ashes. When we scattered him there, I think we must have thought that we'd be there forever. I'm sure otherwise we wouldn't have risked that. He hated conservatories.

ELSIE. Nobody's building a conservatory there, they'd never get planning permission.

SCARLETT. I wish I'd met Stanley. He must have been a lovely man to win you. Will you be okay, Elsie?

ELSIE. We'll soon find out.

> SCARLETT *offers her a hug*. ELSIE *eventually accepts it*.

I think you're going to be an interesting addition to this place.

SCARLETT. I've never been called that before.

ELSIE. I'm sure it won't be the last new thing you're called.
You're going to be all right, Scarlett.

SCARLETT. Will I?

ELSIE. Yes.

SCARLETT. I'll get a curtain.

ELSIE. Yes, you should do that.

SCARLETT. I don't want boys watching me from the bushes.

ELSIE. Nobody wants that, darling.

SCARLETT. Do you want me to give you some peace?

ELSIE. A few minutes' worth. Just a few.

> SCARLETT *nods and goes through to the kitchen*. ELSIE *is by herself. She holds a picture of Stanley. She presses the CD to start playing again. For a moment she is lost in a memory, the music, that first meeting, the dancing. And then it passes. So she sits and waits*.

> ELSIE *watches the room transform around her again. Sometimes she assists, sometimes she is trapped in the memories as it appears* DOROTHY, MARION *or* SCARLETT *play a part in the process. All the while* ELSIE *ages before our eyes. Eventually* ELSIE *is left alone. We are in…*

2016

16th July 2016. Woodside Village Hall. It is now beautifully decorated, a culmination of all that had come before. Bunting, balloons, flowers, photos of ELSIE*'s life, Stanley's photographs. There are newer photos as well, from* ELSIE*'s more recent life.* ELSIE *enters and heads towards the middle of the hall. She is frail. Today is her ninetieth birthday. After a while…*

KATIE (*off*). Elsie?

ELSIE. Can hear you.

KATIE (*off*). Elsie?

ELSIE. Through here.

> *Crashing and bashing. A curse from* KATIE.

> Careful, don't break the door down.

KATIE (*off*). The wheel's stuck! For god's sake. Come on… wheel…

> *A crash and a bang…*

> (*Off.*) Finally.

> *Moments later,* KATIE, ELSIE*'s carer, enters.* KATIE *is pushing a Rollator, she has a rucksack with her.*

> Elsie, what are you doing? You promised me you would stay on the bench. Elsie?

ELSIE. Dot?

KATIE. No, Elsie, you know who I am.

ELSIE. Marion?

KATIE. Elsie.

ELSIE. I'm Elsie.

KATIE. Yes. Now who am I?

ELSIE. Katie.

KATIE. That's right.

ELSIE. Katie. Lots of ghosts.

KATIE. Ghosts?

ELSIE. I got caught up with the ghosts.

KATIE. Do you know where we are?

ELSIE. I know where we are.

KATIE. Where are we?

ELSIE. I've not lost it.

KATIE. For my peace of mind.

ELSIE. Village Hall.

KATIE. And what year?

ELSIE. That's trickier.

KATIE. You know this. You even know what day it is. As it's
    somebody's birthday.

ELSIE. Mine?

KATIE. That's right. And how old are you?

ELSIE. Old.

KATIE. How old's old?

ELSIE. Don't ask a lady that. Older than I ever imagined. Good
    enough?

KATIE. For now.

ELSIE. I have a right to be confused. When you get to my age,
    the amount of faces and names you've heard. There was a
    woman on the radio who called her baby Moroccan.

KATIE. Mariah Carey.

ELSIE. MOROCCAN.

KATIE. Yes, yes, I know.

ELSIE. I would remember that name.

KATIE. Hard to forget.

ELSIE. I'm not Claire Emery.

KATIE. I know.

ELSIE. She needs looking after.

KATIE. You're probably right.

ELSIE. Not even seventy. Walking round the village talking to walls. Her mother was exactly the same.

KATIE. Was she?

ELSIE. You don't remember? She only lived two houses up from your parents.

KATIE. Elsie, I'm twenty-seven. She went way before my time.

ELSIE. Well, you should look after Claire.

KATIE. Then who would look after you?

ELSIE. I'm not as bad as her. She's got no one else. They'll be carting her off to the loony bin if she keeps up the way she is. Very sad.

KATIE. Will you sit in your chair for me, please.

ELSIE. That chair is not my friend.

KATIE. These floorboards are like ice, Elsie.

ELSIE. Ice?

KATIE. Yes.

ELSIE. That's fun.

KATIE. What's fun?

ELSIE. Slipping and sliding. Running on this. Couldn't stop you when you were younger.

KATIE. It's been a long time since youth club.

ELSIE. Go on, you'll have fun. Let go a bit.

KATIE. I think I've grown out of that.

ELSIE. Doesn't matter how old you are, Marion.

KATIE. Elsie?

A moment.

ELSIE. Katie?

KATIE. That's right. Shall we get you sat down in a chair.

ELSIE. I can stand. I can walk. I could even dance if I had someone to dance with.

KATIE. I'm sure you could, just as easily as you could fall over and break your hip. And you don't recover from injuries like that at your age.

ELSIE. What injuries?

KATIE. A broken hip.

ELSIE. I haven't broken my hip.

KATIE. But if you fall. However clued up you are up here. Broken bones you don't come back from that.

ELSIE. I've never broken a bone in my entire life.

KATIE. Well, don't start now. They're one step away from dust.

ELSIE. What are?

KATIE. Your bones.

ELSIE. Nonsense.

KATIE. I've seen an injury like that strike people ten times stronger than you down, Elsie. Signals the end, all that independence – bang, finito! And you're not ready for the end yet, are you, or are you?

ELSIE. How do you think I get anything done at home?

KATIE. You've got rails and ramps.

ELSIE. Eyesore.

KATIE. They're practical.

ELSIE. I don't use them.

KATIE. Well, you can do what you want on your own time. Not when I'm with you though. Or are you happy for me to be hung out to dry if you have a turn? I thought we were friends.

ELSIE. I've met worse than you.

KATIE. Well, that is the highest of praise. When I'm with you do me the courtesy of doing what I'm paid to do. Assist.

ELSIE. Only care about your job.

KATIE. Now that's not funny. I'd never forgive myself. At least meet me in the middle and rest against this.

ELSIE. Even eagles need to perch.

KATIE. Full of pearls of wisdom today, aren't you.

ELSIE. If your grandfather could see you helping me out.

KATIE. Thought we weren't ever going to talk about him.

ELSIE. He'd have shoved me over.

KATIE. It's been said the apple never falls too far from the same tree.

ELSIE. You're not even the same fruit. Timber!

KATIE. That is not funny. I mean it. I'm not laughing.

ELSIE. Katie?

KATIE. No games. I'll strap you in that chair if you won't behave and that's no fun for either of us. Understood?

ELSIE. Understood.

ELSIE *perches*.

KATIE. Now let me put this scart lead where it needs to go without you acting the fool.

KATIE *takes a scart lead out of a rucksack. A moment passes.*

ELSIE. I caught him trying to steal the copper from the boiler in here.

KATIE. I've heard all these stories before.

ELSIE. I said, Edward Reed, putting a potato sack over your head is no disguise. Robbing from his own village.

KATIE. Sooner Paul and I get married the better, finally become something that's not a Reed.

ELSIE. Paul?

KATIE. My fiancé. You have met him.

ELSIE. I know I've met him. He grew up in Hedgeway, didn't he.

KATIE. He did.

ELSIE. Nice to see people out of that village expanding their bloodline.

KATIE. He's not inbred!

ELSIE. What's his surname?

KATIE. You know what it is. Shimwell.

ELSIE. That's what every other family is called up there.

KATIE. I know full well that there are an overwhelming number of Shimwells.

ELSIE. Rest my case.

KATIE. Paul's not inbred.

ELSIE. Big hands.

KATIE. Are you saying he's got big hands?

ELSIE. Who?

KATIE. PAUL?

ELSIE. Paul has big hands.

KATIE. Compared to yours they are.

ELSIE. Put it on my shoulder, thought he was going to crush me.

KATIE. No, you didn't.

ELSIE. Stanley had medium hands. Big hands like that would have been too clumsy for a pilot.

KATIE. Luckily for Paul he's stacking shelves in Sainsbury's in that case.

ELSIE. 'Katie Shimwell'.

KATIE. Don't pull that face.

ELSIE. When is he going to marry you then?

KATIE. Who knows!

A moment.

We talk about a date all the time. But it's so expensive getting married.

ELSIE. We just did it in my day.

KATIE. That's because it was cheap and you had an impetus. Sex.

ELSIE. Just because I wore white down the aisle doesn't mean I was pure.

KATIE. I've seen pictures of Stanley, I would have found it hard to wait too.

ELSIE. You could do it right here.

KATIE. Do what right here?

ELSIE. Wedding.

KATIE. Oh, yeah, that.

ELSIE. In the church. Then here.

KATIE. Copy you.

ELSIE. We had a lovely day.

KATIE. Always wanted it in the church.

ELSIE. Don't see many weddings there now. Used to be every other month.

KATIE. Because nobody young lives here any more! Why are we even talking about this? I'll get all worked up and I'm only meant to be dropping off a scart lead. And you were meant to be waiting outside.

ELSIE. Was I?

KATIE. You know full well you were, but you were being nosy.

ELSIE. I'm not nosy.

KATIE. Oh, come on, you can't dig a hole in this village without you wanting to know what's gone in it. Well, I hope it was worth spoiling the surprise.

ELSIE. Surprise?

KATIE. Don't play the innocent with me, your eyes are bad but they're not that bad.

ELSIE. What surprise?

KATIE. Elsie, what did you think the bunting was up for?

ELSIE.…I put that up?

KATIE. No. No you didn't.

ELSIE. I used to be in charge of bunting.

KATIE. I know, but not today. That bunting's been put up especially for you.

ELSIE. For me?

KATIE. Who else?

ELSIE. The Queen.

KATIE. The Queen?! The Queen's already had her birthday.

ELSIE. We had a lovely day. I put it up for the Queen's Coronation.

KATIE. I am sure you did.

ELSIE. I met Stanley under bunting.

KATIE. I know. In that corner. He asked you to dance and you danced.

ELSIE. His hands never strayed.

KATIE. Wasn't he just the perfect gentleman.

A moment.

ELSIE. That was a long time ago, wasn't it?

KATIE. Only as long as it feels.

ELSIE. It feels a long time.

> KATIE *smiles at* ELSIE.

> I don't deserve bunting. A Queen gets bunting.

KATIE. Well, I think that's how a lot of people see you round here.

ELSIE. Because I'm the oldest in the village. Makes them feel young.

KATIE. I think you're doing yourself a disservice. Didn't put this up for the Queen's ninetieth or the Royal Wedding.

ELSIE. Should have done.

KATIE. Well, you're more important than the Queen, William and Kate then. See, flowers. You've got balloons as well.

> KATIE *hands* ELSIE *a balloon. For a second* ELSIE *is lost in a memory.* KATIE, *now* MARION, *kicks the balloons around.* KATIE *hands* ELSIE *a balloon.*

> …Elsie. Elsie, you'll have to act surprised later.

ELSIE. …Later?

KATIE. Yes, when we come back.

ELSIE. For what?

KATIE. For your party. Marion will kill me if she knows you've seen all this.

ELSIE. Marion?

KATIE. Oh, you did not hear that. That cat wasn't meant to be out of the bag.

ELSIE. Marion is here?

KATIE. You did not hear that from me.

ELSIE. Where is she? Marion?!

KATIE. She's not hiding. She's not in the kitchen.

ELSIE. No?

KATIE. No.

ELSIE. Marion?

KATIE. I'm not lying to you. Fine. Her and Ben have come down for tonight. They've gone to buy more decorations.

ELSIE. Ben's here too! What about the children?

KATIE. Those children are all older than me. All coming. Which is why you've got to forget about everything I've just said. Show me your surprised face?

ELSIE *pulls a face.*

That is terrible. Better practise otherwise you'll get me in serious trouble.

ELSIE. They've really come?

KATIE. Yes.

ELSIE. They've done this for me?

KATIE. Not just them, a lot of the village has played a part.

ELSIE. All for me?

KATIE. It is your ninetieth.

ELSIE. Which you've ruined.

KATIE. That's what you pay me the big money for.

KATIE*'s phone rings. A popular ringtone.*

Marion's ears must be burning.

ELSIE. Is that Marion?

KATIE. Yes.

ELSIE. Marion!

KATIE. Stop that. She's not to know we're here, okay – so quiet. Hello? Hello? Marion, one minute I can't hear you, the reception's terrible. Can you hear me? No. One moment.

KATIE *covers the phone and talks to* ELSIE.

Will you sit in the chair for a moment? Just whilst I'm outside – for me.

ELSIE *nods. She sits in the chair.*

You'll wait here.

ELSIE *nods.*

Hello? Hello? Hello? Better? No. Hello?

KATIE *goes outside.* ELSIE *holds the balloon. She looks around the room. She lets the balloon go. She contemplates getting it. She doesn't. She waits in her chair. She gets out of the chair. She goes and sits down on the seat where her and Stanley first sat. She rubs the seat. She kisses her hand and places it on the seat. She walks back to her chair. She sits.*

ELSIE. Hello?

ELSIE *waits.*

Hello?

ELSIE *waits.*

Hello?

KATIE *enters, rubbing her arms with a dock leaf.*

KATIE. It's a black hole this building! Couldn't get any reception, I ended up having to walk round the back and stand on the wall by the brook. And then I got stung by bloody nettles because it's so overgrown down there. Elsie, are you okay?

ELSIE. Katie?

KATIE. Yes, yes, it's Katie.

ELSIE. Katie.

KATIE. Yes.

ELSIE. I didn't think you were coming back.

KATIE. Of course I was, silly. I'm sorry, I didn't mean to leave you that long.

ELSIE. You wouldn't leave a cup of tea as long you left me.

KATIE. Marion was asking me questions and I couldn't hear her because of the reception. Then the nettles. I was distracted. Sorry.

ELSIE. What would I have done?

KATIE. I was always coming back.

ELSIE. What would I have done?

KATIE. Elsie, I wouldn't leave you.

ELSIE. What would I have done?

KATIE. Elsie – a minute ago you were telling me you could dance round this room.

ELSIE. I was lying.

KATIE. You were not lying

ELSIE. I was cocky.

KATIE. You were not cocky.

ELSIE. I don't want to live forever.

KATIE. Nobody lives forever, you're not that special.

ELSIE. Ninety is far longer than I thought.

KATIE. What's going on? Elsie?

ELSIE. There weren't any ghosts. I know where I am, there should be ghosts.

KATIE. Have you seen *The Conjuring*? Well, I'll save you the trouble, no one wants to be haunted. Come on – let's get you up, this bloody chair, it's making you all mopey.

KATIE *helps* ELSIE *back out of the chair.*

ELSIE. People, moments, they're clouding up.

KATIE. You've had a life. Seen so much, haven't you.

ELSIE. Have I?

KATIE. Don't know many eighty-year-olds that go backpacking round the world.

ELSIE. I spent a year with my ears popping.

KATIE. That's not what the ten photo albums would suggest. Tell me about New York.

ELSIE. I craned my neck from looking up. Entire month there I spent looking up. So big. So shiny. My mouth had never been so wide open. I ate a wonderful amount of flies. Elizabeth had to get me a special pillow, for my neck, to help me sleep. Friendly people. Lovely. Not shy. Elizabeth hasn't fully embraced that. Should have seen how I made her blush when I acted out the *When Harry Met Sally* scene in the diner.

KATIE. Minx.

ELSIE. She has a wonderful life. Her apartment looks over the entire city.

KATIE. No idea why you didn't stay. Looking at the pictures I'd have stayed in Mexico. The beach, the water. Never tempted to stay there, Elsie? In Mexico?

ELSIE. …Mexico…

KATIE. Or any of the other places?

ELSIE. What places?

KATIE. Canada? Argentina? Cuba?

ELSIE. I… I can't remember… what happened?

KATIE. It's in there. Trust me, I hear you tell me all the time.

ELSIE. Everything's fuzzy.

    KATIE *takes a couple of framed photos of* ELSIE's *friends and family and brings them to* ELSIE.

KATIE. Here. You know who they are, don't you.

    ELSIE *stares at the photos. She places her hand on them. Still nothing.* KATIE *ushers* ELSIE *into the corner where Stanley was sat when they first met.*

ELSIE. What are you doing?

KATIE. Have some patience, will you. He was sat in that corner. He tapped his feet. He had a half-pint in his hand. He looked up and your eyes met. He asked you to dance. He never allowed his hands to wander.

ELSIE. They never slipped.

KATIE. He kissed you outside by the brook.

ELSIE. I never told you that.

KATIE. I was only guessing, that's where most of the touching-up took place when I was at youth club.

ELSIE. Some things never change with time then.

KATIE (*re: dock leaf*). Thought these were meant to have some sort of effect. Stings like crazy.

ELSIE. Show me your arm.

ELSIE *takes the dock leaf and starts to rubs* KATIE's *arm.*

Elizabeth had no fear. She'd climb higher in a tree than any boy. She went up and up the oak in our garden. Till I could barely see her. She wanted to see what was over the hill. She said that's where I'm going to live, Mummy. She said that. I shouted her to get down. I must have sounded so angry because she didn't fight me. She threw herself down, branch after branch. She slipped on the last one. The fall wasn't far. We had piles of nettles by its base. No broken bones, no bruises, just head to toe in stings. She was so mad with me, she wouldn't say if this helped.

KATIE. It's working.

ELSIE. It is?

KATIE. I can barely feel them. It's helping.

ELSIE. I miss her.

KATIE. Well, you'll get to see her later, won't you.

ELSIE. This isn't New York?

KATIE. No.

ELSIE. This is the hall?

KATIE. Yes.

ELSIE. Elizabeth left here a long time ago?

KATIE. Yes. Oh man, I'm really not meant to be saying this. Going to ruin another bit of the surprise. Elsie, I'm meant to be setting up the projector.

ELSIE. Projector?

KATIE. So Elizabeth can Skype in.

ELSIE. Elizabeth?

KATIE. Yeah, all the way from New York. I've literally said way too much. You've got to act so surprised later. Marion thinks I've dropped you off with Scarlett.

ELSIE. Marion?

KATIE. That's what she was calling for when I got stung. She was meant to be setting up the Skype but she's stuck in traffic.

ELSIE. Traffic?

KATIE. Blame Michael Ashton. His cows have escaped. Blocked the road. Happened the other week to me. I was sat on the 65 for twenty minutes whilst they worked out what they wanted to do. In the end they just went back to where they'd escaped from.

ELSIE. Cows are always wandering.

KATIE. Yes.

ELSIE. They have soft eyes. Oblivious to the world. Wander into roads.

KATIE. Yes, which is what –

ELSIE. They do that. The cows up at Ashton farm are always escaping.

KATIE. I bet they are.

ELSIE. Wander all over the road. Blame Michael Ashton. Doesn't keep them as well as his father, John always had them under control.

KATIE. Well, because of that, Marion's asked me to set up the Skype connection. So if you don't mind, it will only take a few minutes and then we'll get you home and changed. All right?

ELSIE *nods*.

Shall I take that?

KATIE *takes the dock leaf from* ELSIE. KATIE *helps move* ELSIE *back into the centre of the room*.

ELSIE. Never used to be nettles down there. Path used to be clear.

KATIE. Because there's nobody young left in the village to do any snogging. Either that or the parish council is letting it slide. Only cutting the paths every month now, not fortnightly.

ELSIE. Why is the parish council cutting the path?

KATIE. It's council property.

ELSIE. Never needed the council to cut it before. Somebody from the village would do it. Stanley, Ben did it for a while before they moved. Everyone took it turns.

KATIE. Well, it's the parish council that are supposed do it now.

ELSIE. Your dad should cut it.

KATIE. I'll tell him that. Come on, let me put this blanket over you.

ELSIE *throws it on the floor*.

ELSIE. It's too hot, I don't need it.

KATIE. Well, you didn't have to turn it into a big drama and throw it on the floor. Have you spent all your life throwing things on the floor?

ELSIE. No.

KATIE. Well, why start now?

ELSIE. It's my birthday.

KATIE. What's the blanket ever done to you?

ELSIE. Made me too warm.

KATIE. Your hands are like ice, Elsie.

ELSIE. Blue.

KATIE. Yes, they are blue.

ELSIE. I've always had blue hands. Circulation has always been poor. Stanley used to take them in his. Give them a blow. Rub them. I think I encouraged them to stay blue.

Rubbing and blowing always led to something else.

KATIE. I don't need to hear about that.

ELSIE. Pilots have skillful hands.

KATIE. I'm getting your gloves.

ELSIE. You are not. I am not wearing gloves in July. We had no central heating till 1978.

Snow this deep out here, only logs to burn. I could cope with that, I can cope with this. You do what you've got to do.

KATIE. Well, that's me told, isn't it.

ELSIE. It is. Not having you ruining my birthday twice.

KATIE *smiles and starts to set up the projector.*

Would Paul want to do my garden?

KATIE. My Paul?

ELSIE. The one who hasn't married you.

KATIE. What on earth has made you ask that?

ELSIE. William, Scarlett's boy, used to come round and do the garden.

KATIE. I know he did.

ELSIE. Used to cut the grass. Turn over the beddings. Nothing fancy but he kept it neat. He's stopped coming though.

KATIE. He didn't stop coming, he's at boarding school. It's a bit hard for him to cut a lawn from a hundred miles away.

ELSIE. He told me he loved trees.

KATIE. I'm sure he does. But it was a long way to come to cut your grass.

ELSIE. Paul could do it.

KATIE. He's not a teenager looking for some pocket money. He's got a job. He needs a better one, but I don't think that's the way forward.

ELSIE. I'll pay him.

KATIE. I know you'd pay him. But he's not going to come all this way just to cut your grass.

ELSIE. You come that far to help me out.

KATIE. Well, I'm a fool then, aren't I.

ELSIE. What?

KATIE. I'm a fool.

ELSIE. What?

KATIE. I said, I'm a fool. You just wanted me to say that again, didn't you.

ELSIE. I did hear you the first time. I know lots of people who can't cut their grass any more. Next door they would have someone. Keep it tidy between the lettings. Scarlett is always looking for help. He could do it when he drops you off.

KATIE. I get the bus, don't I.

ELSIE. Don't know why you live there.

KATIE. I didn't choose to live in Newton. It's where we can afford to live.

ELSIE. Doris Christie's cottage was up for sale. The old shop. You should have bought it.

KATIE. It's not that simple.

ELSIE. Want to live here, don't you.

KATIE. Yes. But –

ELSIE. Should have moved in. Little cottage like that, perfect for you.

KATIE. Yeah, well, that's not going to happen.

ELSIE. Born in this village.

KATIE. I know where I was born.

ELSIE. Want to stay you should stay.

KATIE. You know we've tried. You know we can't. Nothing affordable.

ELSIE. No?

KATIE. No!

ELSIE. Could stay with your mum and dad.

KATIE. We're not living with my mum and dad.

ELSIE. I lived with Stanley's parents when we first got married.

KATIE. Yeah, but were Stanley's parents like my family?

ELSIE. Paul's family then.

KATIE. Not living in Hedgeway.

ELSIE. Because of the inbreeding?

KATIE. It's not inbred. All right, it is a little. Even if we did move there or back in with Mum and Dad, is Paul expected to commute back and forth to Sainsbury's for seven and a bit pounds an hour.

ELSIE. Cut my grass as well.

KATIE. That's not funny.

ELSIE. People always need grass cutting. Scarlett always wants someone to look after her garden.

KATIE. It's not like your day, Elsie, where you could live off one wage or people actually could work in the village. Ashton's farm doesn't even have need for seasonal work any more, let alone all year round. It's all machines. And even if jobs did exist you can't live off the wages they'd pay to actually live here. I'm sorry, rant over, I just don't think it's very fair.

ELSIE *stares at a photo of the village from back in the day.*

ELSIE. It doesn't look like this any more, does it.

KATIE. No.

ELSIE. Never used to see a car, now they're on every verge.

KATIE. Of those I went to primary school with, do you know how many still live in this village? Elsie? None.

ELSIE. There's more life in *The Walking Dead* than here.

KATIE. The what?

ELSIE. *The Walking Dead*. It's a TV show.

KATIE. I know it's a TV show. I just didn't know you watched it.

ELSIE. I read about it in the *Radio Times*.

KATIE. Ah, yes, I forgot you're the one person who still buys that. If the village carries on at this rate it won't be long before the school closes.

ELSIE. The school won't close.

KATIE. It will if no one with kids can live here.

ELSIE *looks away.* KATIE *moves some of the equipment. The movement, noise, distracts* ELSIE.

ELSIE. What's that?

KATIE. What do you mean what's that?

ELSIE. That. What are you doing?

KATIE. Have you forgotten?

ELSIE. No.

KATIE. It's okay if you've forgotten.

ELSIE. I chose not to remember.

KATIE. My mistake. I'm doing the projector.

ELSIE. I had forgotten.

KATIE. That's good, I asked you to forget.

ELSIE. You did?

KATIE. Yes.

ELSIE. Why?

KATIE. Because it's your birthday.

ELSIE. This is for me?

KATIE. Yes.

ELSIE. I used to be in charge of bunting.

KATIE. I know, I know you did.

ELSIE *waits…*

ELSIE. You won't let them take me.

KATIE. Who?

ELSIE. I don't know their names. People.

KATIE. The council?

ELSIE. They take people. I don't want to be taken. People get taken.

KATIE. Nobody's taking you.

ELSIE. I don't want to waste away in a home. I want this to be where I die.

KATIE. Why are you talking about that for?

ELSIE. I want to be cremated and put next to Stanley.

KATIE. Stop this talk.

ELSIE. In the roses at the front. Overlooking the village. I want that.

KATIE. You just want to haunt whoever moves in after.

ELSIE. Promise me.

KATIE. Elsie, I can't promise you anything.

ELSIE. Not asking you to turn the incinerator on your bloody self! Not even scatter me with any grace, whoever does it can shake me like I'm salt on chips, I don't care – just make sure that's where I go.

KATIE. You need to speak to Elizabeth or Marion about this.

ELSIE. I'm telling you too.

KATIE. It needs to be in your will, it's no good just telling me.

ELSIE. It's been in my will since the day Stanley went. I just want you to know.

KATIE. Why?

ELSIE. Because who else should I tell? You come every day.
    I want you to know.

KATIE. Okay, I know.

ELSIE. Amongst the roses.

KATIE. Amongst the roses.

A moment.

Elsie… Elsie…

ELSIE. Why do you keep saying my name?

KATIE. I was waiting till after your birthday.

ELSIE. What?

KATIE. The 65 is going to be cut.

ELSIE. Cut?

KATIE. Yes. It's only me on the bus sometimes. They're going to
    reduce it. I don't know how this will be able to work. I have to
    be realistic.

ELSIE. Drive.

KATIE. I can't afford a car.

ELSIE. Stay. Elizabeth's room. Stay there.

KATIE. No.

ELSIE. Not all the time. I'll give you more money.

KATIE. Elsie, I'm not asking you for more money.

ELSIE. I can and I will. Stanley's pension. Savings. I get taken
    care of.

KATIE. I know you do.

ELSIE. You help me, I help you. What do you want?

KATIE. It's not about wanting, Elsie.

ELSIE. I want you to stay.

KATIE. Lucky, aren't you. No debts. Stanley's pension. If Paul was to go right now all I'd be left with his Xbox. Maybe not even that, it's on finance. I hate to think what his credit card looks like.

ELSIE. Both of you stay with me.

KATIE. We're not going to do that.

ELSIE. Why?

KATIE. Many reasons.

ELSIE. Give me one. I'm not going to sit at your door with a glass against it. Both of you stay with me. I don't want to leave.

KATIE. It's not fair to ask me that.

ELSIE. You'll be asked to do a lot worse things in your life time, trust me.

A moment.

I'm alone.

KATIE. You're not alone. You have friends.

ELSIE. Not the ones I'd need.

KATIE. You can get a live-in carer.

ELSIE. No. I need you. Live here for free. Get paid. It won't be forever. You want the house?

KATIE. Elsie.

ELSIE. Can't put a conservatory on top of me. Not build on top of where you put me.

Let me rest in peace.

KATIE. You're tired.

ELSIE. When Elizabeth was born we had a lot of different ages here. I could hear laughter from the school sometimes. I don't hear that now.

KATIE. You don't hear me ringing the doorbell.

ELSIE. I want my home to be a home. I want the person who
lives here to have what I did. I want this place to survive.
I want the school to stay open. Will only happen if you stay.

KATIE. Ridiculous talk. This is all finished, we need to get you
home, you've clearly had too much excitement.

ELSIE. Don't patronise me, girl.

KATIE. We can't take your house.

ELSIE. Not taking – given.

KATIE. But Marion and Elizabeth.

ELSIE. They don't need it.

KATIE. Everyone needs it.

ELSIE. There's other things for them. Live with me. When I go,
you stay. Make it live again. I want you to think about that.

KATIE. Elsie.

ELSIE. Will you do that?

KATIE. You talk to Elizabeth and Marion about it.

ELSIE. I will.

KATIE. That's not why I look after you.

ELSIE. I know.

KATIE. I'm not stealing from anyone. I'm not my grandfather.

ELSIE. I'll speak to them. I will.

KATIE. If it's what you want.

ELSIE. …What I want.

KATIE. Yes, if it's what you want.

ELSIE. What I want?

A moment.

What I want…

Darkness. Music. A swell of light. A comforting pulse that gains more and more energy around ELSIE. *It builds to a crescendo, as for the first time* ELSIE *notices the villagers gathered around her.*

KATIE. Elsie? Look, everyone's here.

ELSIE. Whole village.

KATIE. Yeah. We've got something for you.

ELSIE. For me?

KATIE. We know how sweet your tooth is.

As KATIE *brings out a cake with candles on she leads the villagers in a rendition of 'Happy Birthday'.*

Blow them out then.

ELSIE. Not ninety, are there?

KATIE. No.

ELSIE. I can't.

KATIE. Yes, you can.

ELSIE. Do you want me dead?

KATIE. You can do it. Make a wish.

ELSIE *steps forward.*

She looks around the hall.

The light draws in.

She smiles.

She blows out the candles.

End.

LAST LETTERS HOME

Last Letters Home was first performed at The George Tavern, London, in a production by Drywrite Theatre Company, on 4 June 2009, with the following cast:

REBECCA   Rebecca Whitehead

Director   Vicky Jones

Character

REBECCA, *a twenty-one-year-old northern girl*

Our front door's got frosted glass.
'N' even with this a know from their outline who they are.
There's two of them.
A man and a woman.
Similar height.
Her tall for a woman him average for a man.
'N' they're covered head to toe in this crisp green colour.
'N' as a see this
my heart sinks
cos I know what it means.

–

Andy proposed t'me on the pier at Whitby.
His training base were only a twenty-minute drive away so it
were a place we went to quite often.
We were sat on a bench watching the gulls dive into the water.
I had a Mr Whippy ice cream in my hand
'N' he turned t'me 'n' asked me, 'n' I said yes.
'N' then we just sat watching the gulls and shared the
Mr Whippy.
We were both eighteen.
People who didn't know us that well said it wouldn't last
said we were too young.
Everyone's entitled t'their own opinion
but a knew they were going t'be wrong.
See we never claimed t'be Romeo 'n' Juliet
not some love-struck teenagers who couldn't stop touching
each other.
We were just happy together.
Content.
The thought of him made me smile
'n' vice versa.
It were that simple.
'N' that's why we were going to last.

The service were simple.
Me.

Andy.
My mum.
Andy's parents. Ann 'n' Paul.
Andy's brother: John.
A couple of his mates: Simon 'n' Adam.
'N' two of my mates: Liz 'n' Sarah.

It rained.
But I didn't care.
We swayed together to some music that people would call
old-fashioned.
It were our day
more perfect than I could have ever a wished.

We had three months together before Andy were posted out to
Basra.

–

I open the door.
As I do for a second I close my eyes.
I reopen them
hoping
but they're still there.
The two of them.
All in green.
'N' their uniform
it's so beautifully ironed.
Not a crease.
But their faces
as they see me
as they see how young I am
well, they sort of fold into shapes that I used to draw as a child.

Rebecca Jones, she says.
You want to come in don't you?
Yes, please.

I tell them not to worry about their shoes
and I lead them into the living room.

–

Andy's first deployment lasted six months.
During this time we exchanged a letter a week.

In films when someone reads a letter that's been sent to them
you always hear the writer of the letter's voice.
Andy's voice is very deep.
He has a strong accent.
Stronger than mine.
But his voice is soft.
I try to remember this when I read his letters.
'N' I can do this because he's still fresh in my mind.
When I read about him telling me about the vehicle he's
driving, about the child who told him to fuck off because he
didn't have any Mars Bars to give him, about how hot it is, 'n'
about how he misses me, 'n' how he loves me, 'n' how he will
soon return home to me, it's like he's in the room with me.
'N' as I think this, I breathe in his letters t'catch the smell of his
fingertips and the sweat and fear that makes him smell like the
man I love.

–

They suggest that I sit down.
I think to myself that this mustn't be easy for them
so I do.
I sit on the sofa that Andy and I chose
next to the table with our wedding picture on it
and I say to them: how?

And the man tells me.

Rebecca, I'm very sorry to inform you that First Officer Andrew
Jones died yesterday morning in a roadside artillery attack. He
died instantly.

He does say more but what I'm not sure.
Cos I just stare at the picture of us on our wedding day.
And for the first time since they've arrived I feel the kick of
Andy's unborn baby.

–

When Andy came back from his first deployment we talked
about having a baby.
I want to have a child with you, he said.
I said, I want to have a child with you as well.
And so we spent the next six months trying.

I enjoyed that six months.
But despite our best efforts when he was deployed again we
didn't think we managed it.
I was wrong.
Andy were sent to Afghanistan the second time.
Soon after his letters started to change.
I could still hear his voice
and I could still smell his smell
but the tone were different.
It was tougher what he was seeing.
He was scared
not so much for his safety
but more about what he would miss out on if something
happened.
I tried reassuring him but that seemed to make it worse.
So when I found out I were pregnant I decided not to tell him.
He wouldn't have to worry.
It would be a surprise.
He'd return home to me
to me carrying his child.
'N' we'd be a family.
Just like we talked about.

–

Rebecca?
The woman is sat next to me on the sofa.
Is there anyone you would like us to call?
My mum please, can you call my mum.
Yes, I can.
Thank you.
'N' she does.
'N' twenty minutes later my mum arrives at the door.
He'll never know, he never knew he were a dad.
Shhh, my mum says.
'N' I collapse into her arms.

–

Tell me what you did today.
I did nothing.
You must of done somert.

Well, it were boring.
Perfect, tell me something boring, somert normal.
Okay if that's what yer want.
It is.
I cleaned the oven.
The oven?
I said it were boring.
No it ain't, I can picture you doing that.
You can?
Yeah, what did yer use?
Oven cleaner. Mr Muscle.
Did it work?
Yeah. Spotless.
Like new.
Yeah, I'll send you a picture.
Yeah, do that.
Really?
Yeah. Go on.
Okay.
Becks, can you hear me?
Yeah.
Hello?
I can hear you –
Becks, the line's going funny I can't make you out.
I'm here –
Becks?
Andy?
Look, Becks, if you can hear me –
I can hear you.
I love you. I miss you. And I'll be home soon.
I love you too.
I hope you heard that.
I heard it.
Bye.
Bye.

That was our last conversation.

–

When the two people in the immaculate green suits left the world went into fast-forward.

People came and people went.
Sad faces replaced sad faces.
Black clothes, white flowers became the colours of my
living room.
A brave soul, a wonderful young man, a beautiful person
echoed throughout the house.
Suddenly I'd been a widower for a week.
Mum, I say, what was he like?
Sorry?
I'm scared I won't remember what he were like. I keep trying to
picture him but I can't see him. It's a different face on a
different body –
Shhhh, it's okay.
But I've got to be able to remember him. What will I tell –
You'll remember.
I will?
Of course you will.

A day later I'm sat on the sofa when my mum enters the room.
Somert f'you.
What is it?
Came in the post today. Dated three weeks ago.
'N' I take the envelope from her hand.
'N' across the front is my name 'n' address in a handwriting that
I'd begun to forget existed.
'N' I look at my mum 'n' she says: I'll be in the other room.
I nod at her.

I open it.
'N' I read it.

Dearest Rebecca,

Just a quick note t'thank yer for the picture. It looks good. Like
yer said, brand new. Mr Muscle ever needs a showroom we
could make a fortune.

Seriously though, it's these moments, images, whatever yer call
them, which keep me going.

Thank you.

Always and forever yours
Love
Andy

I close the letter.
Seal the envelope tight.
Trapping every last bit of him in it.

'N' then I smile.

Cos I can still hear his voice.

'N' I put my hand on my stomach.
'N' feel my Andy's child.
'N' I know that whatever his child asks about him I'll be able to
tell them.

A Nick Hern Book

Here I Belong first published in Great Britain as a paperback original in 2016 by Nick Hern Books Limited, The Glasshouse, 49a Goldhawk Road, London W12 8QP, in association with Pentabus Theatre Company

Here I Belong copyright © 2016 Matt Hartley
Last Letters Home copyright © 2016 Matt Hartley

Matt Hartley has asserted his right to be identified as the author of this work

Cover image: iStockPhoto.com/PeskyMonkey

Designed and typeset by Nick Hern Books, London
Printed in the UK by Mimeo Ltd, Huntingdon, Cambridgeshire PE29 6XX

A CIP catalogue record for this book is available from the British Library

ISBN 978 1 84842 622 1